Shampoo and Set

Enjoy!

Best Wishes

Linda Sherlocks

Shampoo and Set

SEVENTY-FIVE YEARS AS A HAIRDRESSER

LINDA SHERLOCK

The Book Guild Ltd

First published in Great Britain in 2021 by
The Book Guild Ltd
9 Priory Business Park
Wistow Road, Kibworth
Leicestershire, LE8 0RX
Freephone: 0800 999 2982
www.bookguild.co.uk
Email: info@bookguild.co.uk
Twitter: @bookguild

Typeset in 11pt Minion Pro

Printed and bound in the UK by TJ Books LTD, Padstow, Cornwall

ISBN 978 1913913 007

British Library Cataloguing in Publication Data.
A catalogue record for this book is available from the British Library.

In memory of our dad Frank and for all the people who have supported our mum Margaret over the years and allowed her to live her dream.

Contents

Prologue		ix
Chapter 1	In the Beginning	1
Chapter 2	The Apprentice	5
Chapter 3	The Sixties	11
Chapter 4	Special Days	15
Chapter 5	Growing the Business	22
Chapter 6	Going Strong	26
Chapter 7	High Days and Holidays	35
Chapter 8	The Seventies and Other Stories	41
Chapter 9	Dad	53
Chapter 10	The Next Stage	56
Chapter 11	The Beginning of the End?	62
Chapter 12	Celebrations	66
Chapter 13	Clients and Friends	71
Chapter 14	A Night to Remember	84
Chapter 15	And So It Goes On	87
Chapter 16	And Then This Happened	93

Prologue

G ood Friday April 2009. Standing in front of the convenience store, it was hard to believe that this was where it all began. It was also where the dream nearly ended before it started. We were on our way to County Monaghan where mum and dad had grown up and where most of our relations still live. Mum had taken much persuasion to close the salon that day. After all, she had a very loyal following of clients, most now in their later years, but who had supported her week in and week out through good times and bad for their hairstyling for over fifty years.

We had left Liverpool early that morning like so many times before to visit the country of our parents' birth, Ireland. This time, one of us was missing. Dad had passed away the year before, although in many ways we had lost him to Alzheimer's slowly over the previous ten years. But it hadn't stopped him going to "work" every day, as he called it.

In 1945, my mum had started living her dream to be a hairdresser and this was where her apprenticeship had started. Eleven years later, she was married to our dad, Frank, who she had met at a dance in Carrickroe Hall. She was a new mum to me and about to start her own hairdressing business over the Irish Sea in the front room of a Lancashire terrace. She was joined by my dad as business flourished in the swinging sixties. How she got the idea is anyone's guess. There were no glossy magazines filled with the latest hairstyles, no products and certainly no highlights or lowlights. Growing up miles from the nearest town deep in the Irish countryside, she was the youngest of six sisters and left without a mother at the age of five. My widowed grandfather sought work in New York –bar work, mainly – to send money home to keep his girls clothed and fed. The tiny thatched cottage surrounded by farmland was cold and desolate on the outside but filled with the laughter of six girls aged eighteen down to five on the inside.

'She's never been like the rest.' The voice of my Aunty Mary echoed in my head as I tried to visualise a hairdressing salon in Aughnacloy, County Tyrone, Northern Ireland, way back then... the end of the war, shortage of money and not exactly the potential to become Beverly Hills.

Chapter 1
In the Beginning

Mum's first foray into hairdressing started one day when she decided to give herself a haircut. She had been left with her sister Bridget while everyone went to the bog to cut turf. Anyone who has ever visited Ireland will know that smell, as it burns even today in open fires. Bored and with few toys to play with, they started by making peg dolls and dressed them with the lining of their sister Eileen's best dance frock, oblivious to the furore which would be unleashed later. The only clock in the house, a giant antique grandfather clock, hovered over them as they twirled the hands until they did not know whether it was night or day. Bridget ran to the tiny shop some twenty minutes away to enlist Patrick to help them to restore the hands of time. Patrick had been to America and had a wall full of clocks. He carefully placed one under his arm for the return journey, taking Bridget by the one hand as she clutched an orange in the other.

'Oranges are for Christmas,' she thought.

But it wasn't even December. In her absence, Mum disappeared into the Upper Room, as it was known, and lurking in a drawer was an object of fascination, brown with rust. A cut-throat razor is never safe in the hands of a five-year-old but Mum found a use for it as her rich brown tresses fell like the pieces of a jigsaw onto the best white candlewick bedspread as she gave herself her first haircut. But there were no mirrors and Mum carried on oblivious until there was the sound of the latch lifting on the front door, the only door.

'Mother of God!' shrieked Aunt Annie. 'What have you done, child?'

Mum knew what she had done when the pixie was produced, a simple knitted hat tied under the chin which she was forced to wear to school the next day. She realised the enormity of what she had done when she had to hide in the Upper Room the next Sunday when two cousins visited from America. They were members of the Catholic clergy, so it was a visit of royal standards. Steaming, freshly made soda bread was lifted from the black skillet pot on the range and served up with newly laid eggs from the hens, butter from the churn in the corner and tea laced with unpasteurised milk from the cows, with blobs of cream floating on the top. Peeping around the door, Mum's curiosity got the better of her as she tumbled into the darkened room, lit only with an oil Tilley lamp.

'Here, share this with your brother,' said Father McKenna to Bridget as he pushed half a crown into her hand. The pixie had been removed and my mum had been mistaken for a boy!

Mum's fascination with hair never left her and at the age of fifteen, she set about in earnest to fulfil her dream. A few neighbours had daughters who had started to train with Mrs Nesbitt in Aughnacloy, serving their apprenticeship for a fee of fifteen pounds, a paltry sum by today's standards but a fortune in 1945.

After leaving school, Mum sought cleaning work in Clogher County Tyrone. Although living on the other side of the border,

Northern Ireland was only a few miles away by the unapproved roads, and with the aid of a bicycle and a good sense of direction, she pedalled her way, living in the big house all week with a few hours at home on a Sunday afternoon. She gathered her wages and kept them in my grandfather's shaving mug high up on the dresser. It was hard-earned money, sweeping concrete floors, scrubbing until her hands were blistered and her knees ingrained with the pattern of the floor. There was the washing-up and the waiting on tables as the wealthy owners and their sons devoured their meals from fine crockery. There were huge dressers to be polished and windows to be cleaned. But Mum had ambition and she needed her apprenticeship fee. Soon, she had enough and went to see Mrs Nesbitt.

'You can start on Monday, but I will need you to bring the money.'

Mum cycled home at twice the speed along the dark, deserted country roads, up the lane to the cottage, careful not to overbalance and roll down the meadow at one side or catch the thorns of the bushes on the other. She dragged one of the rickety chairs over and climbed up to reach for the container embossed with my grandfather's name: Owen McKenna. Gently, her hands shaking with excitement and anticipation, she lifted it down to count it one last time. Peering inside in the dim light of the cottage, she realised it was empty. The money was gone.

But this didn't stop Mum setting off on Monday morning. Perhaps it was the sheer determination which she has had all her life or just pure innocence, but she really expected Mrs Nesbitt to say she could start as planned but she needed the money too as she had a young daughter to feed and clothe. Mum felt humiliated in front of the other girls, most of them neighbours, as she left to return home. Fortunately, Granddad came to the rescue. Seeing her disappointment and wanting to save the family shame, he somehow magicked the fifteen pounds so she could return the next day. So began Mum's first day of the rest of her life.

For the length of her apprenticeship, Mum pedalled each day. Of course, there was still rationing in Northern Ireland as the war had just ended. Homemade butter and eggs laid by the hens were in big demand, so Mum used to smuggle them over the border and sell them to the local shops in the north in order to make some money. She had a special coat with pockets sewn inside and she had to pedal carefully. As she often travelled by what they called the unapproved roads, she was less likely to get caught than if she went through the customs at the border checkpoint, but she was still taking a risk. Little did she know where it was all going to lead and Mrs Nesbitt will never know what she started.

Chapter 2

The Apprentice

Hairdressing is often seen as a glamorous profession, but even today those who go on to achieve fame and fortune have to start at the bottom. Each day, Mum would set off on her bicycle along the back roads on the long journey to Aughnacloy. Porridge for breakfast and a packet of homemade tomato sandwiches or two slices of homemade treacle bread would keep her going. There were no tea breaks, only water. Her first weeks were spent cleaning sinks and scrubbing floors on her hands and knees. Fortunately, she had previous experience. Towels would be washed by hand and put through the wringers, all under the watchful eye of Mrs Nesbitt.

After the first month, Mum graduated to rolling imitation hair onto wooden rollers. Perming would take hours as hair was rolled around metal curlers attached to a machine which ensured the curls became hot. The shampoo was bought, but setting lotion was needed to keep the styles in place as most people had their hair finger waved with pin curls. Linseed oil and borax were boiled in a pan, the liquid strained and poured into bottles and left to cool. Not recommended! Conditioner was almost unheard of and there were very few colours. Inecto and henna gave you black hair and you could be bleached blonde. Grey hairs would be covered with bleach and foil, not dissimilar to today. It was a while before Mum was unleashed on her first real client, but she was allowed to practise first setting and then perming on the other apprentices. It was a long working week from nine until six each day, except Sundays, which were always sacrosanct in Ireland. She learnt how to do finger waves, something which she was still doing in 2019, as well as clip curls. Sometimes, she would practise in the back of the shop on a wooden head before finally being allowed to touch a real client.

After all of that, there were no jobs in the hairdressing world. So, Mum had a temporary change of career as she trained to be a nurse in Omagh, County Tyrone, where she lived in, but she still rode her bicycle home whenever she could, which was an even longer journey. She didn't let her skills fall by the wayside and she often styled the hair of her colleagues ready for a night out.

In the early 1950s, she came to England with her sister Bridget, who was known as Betty. They took lodgings over a grocery shop less than a mile away from where she was to eventually open her salon. A job at the nearby Eaves Lane Hospital saw her combining both her careers; she often did the hair of patients and staff in her lunch hour, all free of charge, but at least she wasn't becoming deskilled. When working nights, she applied for a licence to open a shop in the front room of the house she was buying with my dad in nearby Stratford Road. Getting a mortgage was no easy task. It may seem surprising now to know that it had little to do with their earnings, as they both had secure jobs. My dad was working as a bus driver for Ribble, but they were Irish. They were later to become good friends with the next-door neighbours, Richard and Stella Baxter, and their children Rita and Raymond, but they actually rebuilt the wall between the two houses when they heard who was moving in! Eventually, the licence was granted, but it was only when I was born in June 1956 that Mum became a full-time hairdresser with a new baby in tow.

June 19th 1956 was a momentous occasion. Firstly, I arrived home from hospital at just ten days old. That afternoon, Mum opened the shop, which is still going strong over sixty years later. I was placed in my cot on the fireplace in what had previously been the front room of the 1900s end terrace, which my mum had moved into after she married Dad on February 13th 1954 at Sacred Heart Church, Chorley. They had various lodgers over the years who helped to pay the mortgage, including my Aunty Betty (Bridget), who was still working as a nurse at Eaves Lane Hospital. There was a living room and kitchen at the back with an inside toilet. Upstairs, there were three bedrooms and a bathroom. A large backyard led to a garage and a shed, and this was where I grew up, with ladies coming and going all day. Mum had managed to save up for one dryer, one sink and two chairs. She had purchased a perming machine for the grand sum of £100, but she did get two bottles of rather gruesome-looking and smelly perming lotion for free! Everything had to be paid for in advance. A jar of paste shampoo cost seven shillings and sixpence, and a matching jar of conditioner was similar. It was cold and pink and like a thick mousse or cream. Lacquer was golden yellow and very sticky. It came in a large jar and was poured into a bottle with a spray top. The lacquer used to run down the sides and dry into the ridges of the bottle until I could peel it off. I really don't know what it did to your hair! She also needed scissors, a comb, a brush and a razor. That was the sum total of her equipment. There were also cubicles with curtains for privacy and after closing time, I used to play hide and seek there!

Her first customers were locals like Jean Halton, Mrs Morgan, Mrs Whittaker and Mrs Brown, all known by their more formal names. They had their hair finger waved and clip curled, and they cooed over the new baby. It was Jean who suggested that my mum should have an appointment book. She said that Mum really needed to write everyone down and insisted that she used her first name, but Mum didn't dare tell her that she only had a handful of customers and she was there twenty-four seven anyway.

Mum has often said that it was the local people who supported her the most, although over the years she has had her fair share of nationalities in the shop, including her fellow Irish women. One of the first was a little old lady called Biddy. She wore clogs and a shawl with a long skirt and reminded my mum of the old ladies she saw growing up on a rare visit to town back home in Monaghan. Biddy insisted on sitting on the doorstep as her perm was "taking" and puffed happily from a clay pipe. Having grown up with the perming machine and witnessing it in action, you had to have strong shoulders to have your hair permed in the 1950s. The hair was protected with crepe hair, a type of fine cotton wool which came in long plaits. Pieces would be withdrawn from the plait and placed around the hair, which was then wound around metal curlers. Huge metal clips, which resembled bulldog clips, were heated on the machine and placed around the metal curler to heat the hair. Then you would have to sit with a heavy head until the hair had curled. It was a miracle that women had any hair at all, and the smell of the perming lotion hung in the air long after they had gone home. No wonder Biddy needed a smoke!

One of Mum's first customers was Jean Halton, who lived across the road in Epping Place. Like many women in the 1950s, Jean worked in one of the many mills in Chorley and which could be found in most towns across Lancashire. They worked shifts, usually from 6am until 2pm one week and 2pm until 10pm the following. This worked well for working mothers, as their husbands were often employed in the same factory on the opposite shift, so it meant one of them was at home to care for the children when they came in from school. It made interesting reading in Mum's appointment book, as she often knew which shift they were on and booked them in for their hairdos accordingly.

It was the cotton mills, the towel factory and the slipper factories which gave my mum her first customers, as word spread of the new hairdresser with the little baby who was always willing to fit you in for an appointment and charged reasonable prices. The staff from the hospital remembered the times they had been lucky enough to get their hair done for free and now supported the new enterprise. Customers like Gladys Myers and her mother, Glenda Porter and Mrs Latus, who was like a surrogate grandma to us, as our paternal grandma was in Ireland.

All the Halton girls came to have their hair done, often chased off on a Friday to prepare for the weekend.

'Take a towel, that young woman has a babby to wash for,' their mother would demand.

I must have been a good baby, but then I got plenty of attention from the customers, no doubt. Like clockwork, Mrs Halton had her hair permed in time for every Mother's Day. Her treat was going to bingo and Jennifer, one of the younger ones, would beg her mum to bring home some Belair hair lacquer, which would be poured from a large glass jar and into a plastic bottle. One weekend, her friend Georgina couldn't go out because she had no hair lacquer! Heavily backcombed styles were popular and needed lots of lacquer to hold them in place.

'You'll have no hair left by the time you are forty,' Jean used to warn Jennifer, who to this day still likes lots of hairspray and has a lovely head of hair!

At the age of two, I was actually quite poorly; I spent five weeks in the children's ward of Chorley Hospital and eventually had my appendix removed. My mum and dad were only allowed to visit twice a week. Sister Greenhalgh was especially kind to me. She was guaranteed free haircuts for life. My mum remembers visiting and she told her that I spent all day combing my doll's hair because that is what I thought everyone did.

Business was growing fast and it was decided that a telephone was necessary. Very few houses had telephones in the 1950s and the telephone box around the corner was the only means of communication, especially in an emergency. There was a three-month waiting list, and when it arrived it was a black Bakelite model, which would be much sought after by collectors nowadays. It had a proper dial for the numbers and a little drawer in the bottom where you kept a card with the exchange number on and details of who to contact if the telephone was out of order. It became a lifeline in emergencies for all around and was used to call for the doctor, the ambulance or to track down a runaway teenager. A local printer was employed to design and print some business cards, complete with the telephone number and "Margaret's" was duly established.

Chapter 3

The Sixties

The early 1960s saw changes in what the modern woman wanted when it came to hairstyling. In Chorley, finger waves were still popular with the older clients, but roller setting was becoming popular and, in some cases, the bigger the curl the better. The perming machine was stashed in the cupboard under the stairs and the Rocket Perm was introduced by Clynol. These were such a novelty that they were displayed in the shop window. The bottom part contained the perming lotion and the pointed top part the foam neutraliser, which had to be applied as part of the perming process. In order to be able to use the solutions, Mum had to go off on a course to Manchester, which was almost as big an adventure as going to Aughnacloy on the bike. My dad took her to catch the train each Monday for six weeks. She was joined on the train at Bolton by his cousin's wife, also called Margaret and also a hairdresser. I was looked after by Aunty Betty, who had got married and moved to Preston. My dad had to go and pick her up before my mum left. There was always a present from Aunty Betty or from Mum to soften the blow of her going, even though she was back in time for tea. One evening, they caught the wrong train and ended up miles out of their way in Southport, which led to great difficulty getting back to Bolton.

'We'll have to ring Frank and let him know what has happened, as he will be waiting for me at Chorley and Linda will be having a fit!' my mum protested to Margaret, but she just laughed it off.

'He'll think we're stupid. We'll just have to wait for the next train.'

Eventually, they managed to get back on track and arrived home many hours later than planned.

A certificate was awarded and is displayed proudly until this day. The perms were softer and less harsh for the hair, but Clynol would not sell you their Warm Air perm unless you had completed their six-week course where they taught you how to section the hair and the importance of timing the perming process, especially as heat was applied. A blue, elasticated hat was put on the completed perm and the head was steamed under the dryer for ten minutes. There was also Clynol Cold Wave for those who didn't like the heat or had coloured hair, but they were both a far cry from the heavy rods applied to Biddy's head! Hair colours were also changing, and the bleached-blonde look was very much in vogue and inspired by stars such as Marilyn Monroe and Diana Dors. There were tints such as Harmony which could be bought to add different colours. Eventually Clynol introduced their Viton range and the company rep ran a course in the shop one Monday morning and a number of customers got a free colour for trying them out.

Growing up in a hairdressing salon did have its advantages. As I could toddle into the shop, my mum could keep an eye on me, and I wasn't short of presents when it came to Christmas and Easter. Catherine McQuillan, now Cath Murphy, was a young, single Irish girl who worked in Melias' grocery shop in town. She often bought me smocked dresses from Kennedy's shop, which must have cost a fortune as they were the 1960s Lancashire equivalent of today's designer clothes. A German lady, Mrs Gregg, was also a customer but not a millworker. Instead she could tailor make dresses for me and my doll from pieces of nylon purchased from Lawrence's mill where Jean Halton worked. They had the foresight to produce synthetic fabrics alongside the traditional cotton. The material was just too good to resist at two shillings a piece and my current favourite doll, Glenis or Lorraine, would have a matching dress. One had red rosebuds with a red bow at the neck and Glenis had one just the same. Seeing hairdressing every day made me want to practise it too. One day, I insisted on giving Glenis a haircut. My mum told me that it would never grow again, but I insisted it would. It didn't, of course, but I had to learn the hard way. One day, dressed to the nines, I was playing in the shop as my mum worked away.

'Whose is that gorgeous golden curl lying on the floor?' asked one of the customers, who was waiting for her perm to neutralise.

'I don't know,' replied my mum.

But she soon found out. It was mine; as I was experimenting with the hand-held clippers which she used to tidy up necks I had managed to take off at the roots one of my long, red ringlets. I had obviously inherited my mum's skill for cutting hair at an early age, as I must have been about four years old at the time.

Often, I would sit on the knee of someone having their hair done. They didn't mind. The front of the shop was quite safe as we had a wall, a hedge and a wooden gate. I was able to play outside and chat to people going past, who would give me toffees. My large Silver Cross pram, complete with baby doll, would often have little old ladies waving across, thinking it was a real baby that I was taking care of while my mum worked. I can remember one lady called Kathleen helping me to make paper chains from copies of *Woman* magazine. They were happy times and my mum was always there for me.

Chapter 4

Special Days

One day which stands out in my mind is the day of Princess Margaret's wedding to Antony Armstrong-Jones. It was May 6th 1960 and it was business as usual at the salon. Connie Mawdsley was booked in for a perm.

'Your Linda's very quiet,' she commented. 'Has she fallen asleep?'

I may have been just coming up to four years old but when my mum checked in the living room, I was mesmerised by the black and white TV pictures which were being beamed into homes around the country from Westminster Abbey as twenty million people shared their great day. The princess, dressed in white silk and diamond tiara, was followed by eight bridesmaids including Princess Anne, whose hairstyle I tried to copy after the ceremony. But only after I had played at weddings, clipping one of my mum's overalls to my head as my pretend veil, having managed to pull it down from the hook as it hung in the cupboard under the stairs. It was the start of my fascination with weddings, fuelled by the numerous events which my mum helped to style hair for in the subsequent years.

Similar to weddings and which created one of the busiest weeks of the year in the salon was the Annual Church Walking Day. These were a popular event in Lancashire in the 1950s and 1960s and although they still exist today, they are generally on a much smaller scale. All the local churches would walk from their parishes and through the town centre. The little children, boys and girls, would be dressed as if they were going to a wedding. The mums would have been planning for months what colour their church would walk in that particular year and yards and yards of material would be purchased so that matching dresses could be made by mums and aunties and grandmas and anyone who was handy with a sewing machine. Pretty headdresses and white shoes and socks completed the outfit and the florists had a field day as the little girls carried posies or baskets of flowers. Not to be outdone, the boys usually had smart trousers, white shirts and a flower which complemented the colour of the girls. They walked in rows, held back by coloured ribbons, with an equally well-dressed adult at each end to guide them. It would be another outing for the adults' wedding guest outfits or an excuse for a new frock. The men, in their best suits, would carry the banner proclaiming the name of the church and they would often have to battle against the wind as they paraded through the town. The Brownies, Guides and other uniformed organisations made up the procession, along with a marching band or two. The streets would be lined with people who had placed their deck chairs by the roadside, early in the day, to mark their spot. Of course, all this revelry led to many more hairdos. Some of the older ones, who often walked with the Mothers' Union, came on the Friday to avoid the pandemonium of the little children and not-so-little stroppy teenagers on Saturday morning.

'You'll not walk lady if you don't get that hair done!' could be heard as Alice Jones was ushered into the shop by her ever so forceful mother, her screams having been heard since she was halfway down the ginnel leading to Stratford Road. Styles varied from shampoos and sets, even for the teenagers, or finger waves with or without ringlets, dependent upon the length of hair available. I used to always want to walk on Walking Day, but Catholics didn't join in, as it was usual for them to walk around their own church or to scatter petals as they walked in the month of May in honour of Our Lady. But one year I did walk, in a sort of a way.

'Our Linda's walking on Saturday,' Aunty Betty confided in the appropriately named Mrs Blessed whom she worked with at Eaves Lane Hospital.

'But I thought you were Catholics?'

'Well, yes, but Linda won't bother as long as she gets to put her fancy frock on and carries a bunch of flowers.'

Very kindly, she offered to make me a posy, so on Saturday I just had to have my hair done. I sat in all my finery in the shop for hours before. I hogged the dryer until the last minute, as I was part of the big day, or so I thought.

'Is she walking?' was the question of the day.

'Yes,' my mum would reply.

'I didn't know your lot walked.'

'Well, we don't, but she is,' my mum answered.

We waited until we could hear the bands in the distance and my dad took me up onto Eaves Lane, where I held tightly to his hand as I walked down Stump Lane and everyone stepped out in style. Fortunately for him, when I got to Billy Butcher's shop, I realised that I wasn't far from home.

'I want to go and see my mum,' I decided.

My ambition to join in had been fulfilled, so I headed back home to do my doll's hair for the weekend.

Before my brother Adrian was born, it was decided that we would get a dog. Kathleen, who lived further along Stratford Road and was a client, had poodles and put my dad in touch with a reputable pet shop in Preston. We went along one evening and I chose a little white poodle puppy called Kim. I was warned to keep him in the living room until after he had been immunised, but I was keen to introduce him to the shop. He became part of the scene and he would sit on the client's knee under the dryer. He seemed to be able to sense those who were dog lovers. In this day and age of health and safety, I suppose it would be frowned upon. Ironically, my mum became allergic to dogs, but she was still heartbroken when Kim had to be put to sleep.

Weddings were also very much to the fore, especially in the summer months. I loved weddings and as many brides had their dresses made, either by the local dressmaker or the mother of the bride, I was often on the receiving end of the leftover pieces of material, which came in very useful for dressing my dolls. In October 1962, shortly before my brother was born, one of my mum's regulars, Teresa, was getting married. It really was touch and go whether the bride, bridesmaids and most of their family would get their hair done that Saturday, but fortunately Adrian didn't arrive until about 10pm the following foggy Tuesday night. He was born at home and reminiscent of a scene from the popular BBC drama *Call the Midwife*, he didn't arrive until shortly after my mum had styled the midwife's hair! At that time, new mothers were supposed to stay in bed for ten days and the doctor visited several times. What he didn't know was that once he had gone, Mum was out of bed and helping out in the shop.

I was delighted to have a baby brother, although I had been hoping for a sister. My dad took me to Rigby's newsagents on Eaves Lane and bought me a talking doll. I had six different ones before I got one which actually worked. She was called Chatty Cathy and you pulled a string in her back and she had a number of stock phrases. While I was there, I insisted that we buy the new baby a present. I had a Yogi Bear money box and if any of the ladies gave me some money, I put it in. There was a

Huckleberry Hound one, so we got that for him. When we got back to the shop, I put them side by side in between the two sinks. When my mum came down one day after the doctor had gone, she insisted that I put them away as it looked like I was begging. We had an intercom linking the sitting room and the shop so that my mum and dad could hear Adrian if he woke up or if he cried. I can remember singing "Away in a Manger" that first Christmas and I had completely forgotten that they could hear me in the shop. There were some older ladies who thought it was very sweet!

At one stage, I decided to open my own salon in my bedroom. I "borrowed" my mum's open and closed sign and put it on the window. I made a price list and invited my schoolfriends to bring their dolls to have their hair styled. I don't think I went so far as to charge them, but the business didn't last long as it caused confusion in the neighbourhood. People thought my mum had opened another salon upstairs, so she made me close it down. On a visit to Ireland one year, I got a doll with purple hair. She would be the height of fashion now, but it just didn't seem right to me. One day, my mum had some brown hair dye left over in the bowl, so I decided to colour it. I was amazed when it came out a perfect colour. I used to perm and set their hair as well. Customers didn't mind when I commandeered a dryer for a while, but my mum wasn't too pleased when she had a shopful of wet heads. As so many had shampoos and sets in those days, it was like a conveyor belt system as they took their place under the dryers in order. As one was ready to comb out, another one was ready to go under. It's no wonder that my mum and dad got through maybe thirty or forty clients in a day.

A few years later, Rosie had the most beautiful peach satin material for her bridesmaids and for herself a lovely material with a raised bobble, which I put to good use for Tressy, the doll whose hair did grow, when she was being prepared for her wedding. I had learnt how to sew from my mum, usually when she was absolutely worn out on a Saturday night when I insisted Sindy or one of her pals needed something new for the weekend. I made a wedding dress for Barbie with an underlay of white satin with the bobble fabric on top. I did their hair, of course, and picked some flowers from the garden at the house next door to the shop, which my mum and dad had bought in 1963 to convert into two flats. It was almost my birthday and I had ordered Ken, Barbie's boyfriend, who was new in from America, as a birthday present. Now we were never rich growing up as hairdressers in the 1960s, but we always got what we asked for, within reason, for birthdays and Christmas. But Ken did not materialise on June 9th and I was bitterly disappointed. I had the wedding party lined up on the chair at the back of the shop, just waiting for the groom.

'We couldn't get one,' Mum explained, 'so she will have to marry Adrian's Action Man instead.'

With a scar on his face and hardly a decent outfit to wear, I didn't think he was the best match for the elegant Barbie, with her blonde bobbed hair, slim figure and new rig out.

'Put the red guard's outfit on. After all, the royals usually get married in their fancy uniforms,' was my mum's solution to keep me quiet while she got on with her sets and perms for the day.

Sometimes, we were invited to weddings, but it was often difficult to attend, especially if they were on a Saturday morning, as often people got married earlier in the day in the 1960s than they do now. One wedding which we did enjoy was that of Cath and Pat Murphy. It was on Easter Monday 1967 and Mum opened the shop specially to do everyone's hair. I can remember skipping along Stratford Road to the grocer's shop, which was closed for the bank holiday, and being really excited, as I loved weddings. Later that afternoon, we dressed up in all our finery and set off for St Joseph's Church, where we had our photographs taken. The reception was over Hall's shop on Eaves Lane, which was a popular venue for weddings. Partway through, Adrian got bored, so my dad took him downstairs, as they sold toys. He got a *Man from U.N.C.L.E* gun, which would be frowned upon nowadays, but it was quite acceptable then. He had great fun playing with it.

Chapter 5

Growing the Business

As the business grew in the early sixties and with me about to start school, my mum realised that she needed extra help, but she couldn't afford to pay an assistant, so she decided that she needed to look a little closer to home. My dad had worked for many years as a conductor and a driver for Ribble Bus Company, but the unsocial hours after my arrival in 1956 led him to change direction, and he got a job with Hills' Bakery as a delivery driver, visiting shops and cafes all around the area with bread and cakes on a daily basis. Although it was often an early start, he finished by mid-afternoon and was around to help at home. As he wasn't earning a great deal and my mum was having to turn clients away, she suggested that he gave up his job and learn hairdressing. Now there were very few male ladies' hairdressers in the 1960s and even less in a small Lancashire town like Chorley. I have often thought that if only I had a pound for every person who assumed that my dad was a barber, I would be rich, and in my teenage years especially I found it difficult to explain what my dad did for a living, which seems strange in the twenty-first century.

My dad joined the business, starting by helping with the towels, answering the telephone and making appointments before graduating to washing hair and generally getting to know the business. He went on courses in Manchester and the rest he learnt from my mum. He also came in useful for taking me to and from school and home and back at lunchtime, as very few children stayed for school dinners. Nowadays, hairdressers tend to wear their own clothes or just look trendy, but my mum and dad had nylon overalls made and they complemented each other. I remember a short, navy version for my dad and a similar one trimmed with white for my mum. Next time it was brown with their names embroidered on them – Margaret and Frank – as if the customers didn't know them! Looking back, having dressmaking skills in the sixties must have been quite lucrative, especially with so much material being produced in Lancashire.

My dad soon built up his own list of clients, but at the same time, my mum and dad would work as a team. His popularity increased when on hot summer days he would often treat the clients to an ice cream when the van rolled up outside. I am not quite sure what it did for the profits! Of course, Adrian and I would always get an ice cream treat. Mrs Pilkington was a lady I remember well, and she used to bring me a bag of sweets and chocolates on a Saturday morning. She would slip them into the window cupboard and then I would find them. She had a daughter called Rosemary, so when I got a baby doll, I gave her the same name in her honour. It is little wonder that I grew up with a sweet tooth.

As the business grew, so did my brother, and while I would quietly read a book, play at school or do my doll's hair, he was harder to occupy. He wasn't keen on nursery and he only went in the afternoons, but we had our pretend nanas to take care of him. There were two in the main. Mrs Mullen, or Ma Mullen, as she became known, lived across the road and often Adrian would be taken across with a tin of beans for his tea while she made toast on the fire. Alice Latus was another.

'Is your Linda playing weddings again?' asked Alice one week.

'She's always playing weddings and she would love to be a bridesmaid.'

'Leave it with me,' confided Alice.

On October 26th 1963 at St George's Church, Chorley, I was one of four bridesmaids for Barbara and Derek Latus. Of course, the wedding party was booked in for Saturday, and at long last I was a genuine customer with a proper occasion to attend. The dresses were made by Mrs McDonald, who lived next door but one to Alice and her husband Jimmy in Geoffrey Street. I just loved that dress. It was true Little Bo Peep style, and I had my white shoes and socks, white gloves, and a ring of lilac artificial flowers in my newly coiffured hair. Along with a posy of white carnations, I felt like a princess. Barbara had also given me a lovely silver bangle, which I have to this day and which I took with me when I attended their golden wedding party in 2013. Fortunately, the shop closed early on Saturdays, with the first customers arriving shortly after 7am, so when I arrived at the church, my mum, dad and Adrian were there.

The friendship didn't end there, as I remember my mum combing up Barbara's hair one Christmas morning when she wanted it to be extra special. Every time they went on holiday, they always brought us presents. Once it was a plastic handbag with scenes of Great Yarmouth. I think Alice, Jimmy, Derek and Barbara must have been the first people I knew who went to Spain for their holidays, which was most unusual. They brought me back a gold coloured bracelet with mother of pearl. I still have a book which they bought for me at Christmas 1965. They could never have imagined that those gifts would be remembered long after they had gone, as out of the four only Barbara survives.

As we had so few relations in England, except for Aunty Betty and some cousins on my dad's side, it was the customers who often helped out at times of crisis. When my dad had to go into hospital for two weeks in June 1963, my mum was left with a seven-year-old, a young baby and a business to run. The customers would often help to keep us amused. Dad wasn't even in the local hospital, as he had a problem with his eye, a problem which would now probably be dealt with as an outpatient. The only way to visit him was by bus, so with Adrian left with one of the pretend nanas and with me in tow, Mum would set off a couple of times a week to visit. But it was more complicated than that because children under fourteen were not allowed in, so Alice Goldsworthy came with us and as luck would have it, Aunty Betty was now living with her husband Clifford and her young family across from Preston Royal Infirmary. Alice and I stayed there while my mum visited and then we would set off for home.

Mrs Marrow was another who was good to us. She looked after the children of our family doctor, so she came highly recommended. She would take Adrian, especially when my dad was in hospital, and generally help out. Her daughter, Anne, was a teenager, and I remember being fascinated by her. She gave me some of her Noddy books and showed me how to cut cheese slices so that they fit exactly on a cream cracker! Another customer brought me a book and even brought some shoes from a local shoe shop so that I could fit them on and choose a pair. We really did miss our dad, but everyone rallied round to keep us happy.

Chapter 6

Going Strong

———

Of course, meeting so many different people, all ladies, did bring its problems.

Many of them wore hearing aids, having become increasingly deaf after working with the looms in the cotton mills. These were not the sophisticated miniscule devices which we know today. These were very large and had a long, twisted wire leading from the earpiece to goodness knows where. Daisy had spent many years working in Talbot Mill and was a regular. My mum accidently cut through the wire while perming her hair. Fortunately, she failed to notice, which says a lot about the effectiveness of hearing devices in the 1960s. She never complained. Nellie was another weekly customer.

'Now before you start, Margaret, I've been going to Madame Edith's and I have these blackouts. If I have one, don't send for the ambulance. They did that at my last appointment and I was at the hospital for hours before they sent me home. If it happens, just put me in your other room and let me sleep it off.'

Everything went well for many appointments until one day, it happened very early one Saturday morning. She went out like a light, much to the dismay of the other customers.

'It's OK,' my mum reassured them. 'She warned me what to do if this happened.'

My mum and dad took her and put her on the settee at the back where we lived and covered her with a blanket. Everything went well until Adrian came down from bed. 'What's she doing on there? I want my breakfast and to play with my cars on the table!'

This was the routine on a Saturday, as we had a very heavy folding table which we put in front of the fire in the wintertime as it was so much cosier than the kitchen table in the back. Nellie was moved to a nearby armchair while Adrian tucked into his bacon butties and played with his toys. After a while, she came round and my dad gave her a drink of water so that he was able to finish her hair. Off she went, as if nothing had ever happened. I used to love going down to her house for a treat on a Friday evening as she sold chocolate from her sideboard. She would open the drawer and let me choose and chat to me while I decided. She always had a changing range of products so there was something different every week. Thankfully, she never passed out again.

Nellie wasn't the last person to pass out. With one or two clients, it was a regular occurrence and occasionally the ambulance had to be sent for, but mostly my mum got to know them and managed to bring them round with a cup of tea and a biscuit. Sadly, one lady did pass away under the dryer. One minute she was fine and the next she was gone. It was a very sad day and a shock for everyone.

On the other hand, there were often humorous moments too. One day, a rather quiet Winnie came in. She was usually very bubbly, so my mum was somewhat puzzled but didn't comment.

'Margaret, will you highlight my hair?'

'Yes, I have time for that.'

She fell asleep under the dryer and my mum backcombed her hair and sent her off. The next week, she came in as usual and took her place on the chair at the washbasin.

'Tell me something, Margaret, did you highlight my hair?'

'Yes, Winnie, you asked me to do it last Saturday. Why?'

'Well, to tell you the truth, I had been for a drink or two when I came in last week and I was a bit hungover all weekend, so I never looked in the mirror. It was only when I went to work on Monday that they all said how nice it was, but I couldn't remember a thing.'

I think Winnie was a bit more careful when she went to the pub after that. However, it wasn't the last time that her Friday nights out got her into trouble. Shift dresses were the fashion, so with her sister Mavis they ran up a couple out of some brand-new white sheets which their mother had stashed away in case anyone was ill or, worse still, had died and they had to send for the doctor. As if that wasn't enough, they decided to dye them pink with the aid of the brand-new washing machine which their dad had saved for months to buy from his wages earned working in the coal mine. The two girls went off to the local dance hall, dressed to the nines and were much admired. Everything was well until Monday, when their mum decided to do the weekly wash and everything came out pink! The dye was still in the drum of the washing machine as they hadn't rinsed it out. That is one household that never forgot their first taste of modern wash-day technology.

My mum was also unrecognisable one day when she had a change of hairstyle. Adrian was having his afternoon nap and I was at school. Now as a hairdresser, you are often the last to get your hair done, so, seizing the moment, my dad volunteered to cut my mum's hair and perm it. She was transformed from having a 1960s French roll or pleat to a softer, curlier style. Everything was well until Adrian woke up. He roared the place down. Such had been the transformation that he didn't recognise his own mother!

Another occasion when my mum looked rather different was when she decided to model one of the curly wigs which she had just started selling. It seems rather strange that she would want her customers to have these, but they often had them set too. Iconic country singer Dolly Parton has often commented that she has no idea how long it takes to do her hair as she is never there, so I suppose there are still hairdressers who find this is another source of income. They were more a fashion statement rather than a necessity, as nowadays there are some very good wigs and specialist suppliers, especially for women who have alopecia or may have undergone chemotherapy. The 1960s wigs came in a variety of colours, looked most unnatural and had a large tight band of elastic all the way round. They made their heads sweat as they sat in the club on a Saturday night, as well as leaving a red mark all around the head. The price of glamour! I can remember trying them as a little girl and quickly casting them aside, deciding to remain a natural redhead. The wigs were stored on individual polystyrene faceless heads on the shelf which still runs along the front of the shop over the mirrors.

One weekend, my mum spent hours washing and setting about ten of these ready for collection midweek. The telephone rang and my dad spent ages chatting to his mate about football and was oblivious to the fact that our pet budgie, who was enjoying a bit of freedom in the sitting room next to the shop, had decided to follow him in. Seeing all his new friends, he decided to land on them one at a time, and with polystyrene being so light, they ended up on the shop floor. When my mum came in, it looked as if there had been a massacre. There nearly was when she realised who had caused the commotion. She had to spend Sunday afternoon redoing them all.

We sold a variety of extras in the shop in those days, as there were few shops, which sold hair accessories. We sold frilly mobcaps which came in individual packets and sold for three shillings and sixpence. They came in lovely pastel colours and were beautifully finished off. I nearly always managed to choose a pink one whenever any new ones came in, so that was the profit down the drain! Customers usually treated themselves to one whenever they had a perm. Others preferred hair nets, just like the ones worn by the famous *Coronation Street* character Ena Sharples. We also stocked nylon hooded scarves which tied around the neck and can often be seen worn by characters in 1960s films.

Rain mates were another standby, as no-one wanted to get their hair wet, having spent over an hour having it done. We once had some which came in a little plastic container which you could attach to your handbag so you were never caught in a shower. To this day, many of the customers have one in every bag, so they were a good invention even if they don't look particularly glamorous. The nets I liked the most were very fine, invisible and had tiny beads. I loved having my hair in a bun with this around to make it stand out. I think I was the only one at primary school who had access to these.

Combs were another popular line and came in a box or on a card in various pastel colours. I always had one of those too so that I could do my doll's hair as well as my own. I remember the high quality of the brushes and they lasted for years. My mum and dad had "reps" that would call and supply them or they would go to Halsteads in Bolton to stock up. Nowadays, all these things can be bought cheaper on the high street, so there is little profit for the hairdresser and it can often take a long time to move the stock.

All these extras helped to pay the overheads. At that time, my mum used to rent towels from a company who supplied local hairdressers. It saved on washing and drying, especially with two young children to look after, as well as working long hours. We had white ones for general use and black ones for colouring and perms. This worked fine for a while, as every salon had their own supply, but when she started to get other people's towels which were not very well looked after, my mum decided to supply her own. She sent my dad around the corner to the Towel Factory and he came back with a huge bundle on his shoulder, so high all she could see peeping out was the end of his nose and his Eric Morecambe glasses! They were two shillings each and superb quality. She even resold some of the white ones to any mothers-to-be, as they were exactly what they needed for the new baby. In the early days, I remember clients bringing their own towels and taking them home to wash themselves. I used to love looking at all the different patterns, especially stripy ones.

Sometimes the customers would try to make a bit of extra money and ask if they could sell to the others. I remember a craze for what can only be described as fluffy rugs. Janice who came in supplied off cuts of wool with a backing and you glued these to a large rug-shaped piece with thick white glue. My dad had a go and we had one in red. It was fine until Kim the dog discovered that he could lift the pieces off with his teeth and we had a bald rug!

Of course, some customers liked to do their own hair in between, especially to save money, and women could often be seen walking around in their rollers with a scarf tied round as they were preparing for a night out. Although most men went to the barbers to have their hair cut, sometimes my mum and dad would trim and style the hair of the husbands and sons of the regulars. Bob has been coming since he was a little boy living around the corner and he retired many years ago. But one man who thought he would save money but lived to regret it was Alf. They started to advertise a device for home cutting which they demonstrated at regular intervals during the most popular programmes on TV and which made cutting hair look like running a knife through butter. Alf had noted this and decided it could be a good long-term investment. But he soon had to get the missus to come crawling to my mum.

'Hello, Margaret, it's Eileen from Coppull. Do you think you could cut my Alf's hair or at least what's left of it?'

'What do you mean?' enquired my mum, thinking he must be recovering from some kind of illness.

'Well, he sent for some of those clippers they've been advertising on the telly. When they came, he plugged them in, but he didn't bother about using any of the fittings and started cutting his hair. He reckoned he'd watched you and Frank often enough and that it looked dead easy. But he got halfway up his head when they got stuck and they wouldn't move. He kept asking me to pull the plug out, but what with my arthritis I couldn't get down, Margaret. You know what our Alf is like; he didn't realise that he could switch them off at the handle, so by the time I got them unplugged he had at least three bald patches all across his head. He's got long strands and clumpy bits.'

'Well, what do you want me to do about it?'

'You'll just have to shave it all off and he'll have to let it grow again.'

So that was what she did. He had boasted to his wife that any fool could do what my mum did and he even had ambitions to do other people's hair. There was something about the whole incident which made Alf realise that hairdressing is not as easy as it looks.

Alf wasn't the only one who had been influenced by the adverts. Phil had twin boys and they had always been as good as gold whenever they had their hair done, until one fateful day when they arrived with their mum. The two four-year-olds seemed reluctant to come in and were screaming outside.

'Can you cut their hair?' was the frazzled mum's request.

'Well, I can't cut it if they are crying like that. They aren't usually any trouble. What's happened?' my mum wanted to know.

It seemed their dad had been watching my mum too and decided it was a doddle. The next-door neighbour had frightened the daylights out of the two little boys when they had had a similar experience to Alf.

'Can you not pin them down and do it?' their mum wanted to know.

'Certainly not,' my mum informed her, and that was the last that she saw of them.

Home colouring is also an area open to disaster, although products have improved more recently. But in the early days, my mum and dad were often the first port of call when it had gone wrong.

Joan put a colour on one Saturday morning and decided that she would get on with the cleaning while it was "taking". Her son arrived and decided to have a late breakfast.

'What have you done to your hair?' was his first response.

'I've put a colour on. Why, what's wrong with it?'

'Well, you'll be alright down at the Rovers this afternoon because it's bright blue!'

She was soon on the telephone and confessed what had happened.

'Come down and I'll sort it out Joan,' my mum sighed.

She arrived some twenty minutes later with a tea towel round her head, turban-style. Some of the customers thought she had had a different kind of accident.

'I never thought to look in the mirror. I just put it on and got on with the cleaning.'

Thankfully, the addition of a brown colour soon restored Joan to her more natural self. But she paid twice for her mistake and never tried home colouring again.

'I'll leave it to the expert next time.' She laughed as she closed the door behind her.

Ironically, nowadays no-one would bat an eyelid at Joan if they met her in the street with blue hair. In fact, they would probably pay her good money to do theirs for them!

We were always busy in the shop, so quite why my dad decided to introduce Green Shield Stamps is a bit of a mystery. They were an incentive for people to shop with you and were very popular with drivers who were given them with petrol, particularly if they weren't paying for it. You had to stick them in books and then when you had the correct number of books, you could exchange them for goods chosen from a catalogue. The shopkeeper had to buy them, so whether they made good economic sense for my mum and dad I suppose I will never know. We collected them and the highlight was going to Wigan to the Green Shield Stamp shop to exchange them. I had umpteen pen and pencil sets using them. Once, as a publicity stunt, Batman and Robin came to Wigan in the Batmobile. Adrian was about five at the time and Batman-mad, as the TV programme was at the peak of its popularity on Saturday and Sunday evenings. We didn't tell Adrian why we were going, so he had a great surprise when his heroes went whizzing by. The town was in chaos, as there were excited children everywhere with equally excited parents. No health and safety then! It wasn't even the real actors, just someone dressed up, but it is a day we will always remember.

Chapter 7
High Days and Holidays

Holiday times were always extra busy. Christmas brought works parties and special nights in the local clubs. Add two excited children and you had double trouble. The older ladies would come in and remind us about Father Christmas and of course we would think his arrival was imminent when it may have been days away. I can remember receiving a Huckleberry Hound annual, which had obviously been put away for Christmas, just to keep me quiet. We would get some lovely presents from the customers and until this day I have a nursery rhyme book which I was given by Mrs McGreal when I was just six years old. Another lady, Miss Thornton was an English lecturer at the local teacher training college for mature students. She used to buy us the most beautiful books, which again I still treasure. The first "proper" book which I ever read was *Pinocchio*, which she bought for me one Christmas. "Irish" Nora used to always call on Christmas Eve with two boxes of Terry's All Gold. My mum used to work so hard, especially on Christmas Eve, that she often spent the festive season flat out with what we called flu, which would now be labelled a seasonal virus.

Easter brought lots of Easter eggs. Good Friday was one of the busiest days, as many of the teenagers and their parents would climb Rivington Pike. The girls would all want their hair set and I would look on in envy at their sixties-style "sticky out" skirts. Special buses would run and it would be a great day out, with the climb being of religious significance as well as a fun day out. In the morning, many of the women would have been on Chorley market to buy fresh fish from Johnny Burr. It would be the only stall which was open that day, but it was a local tradition. In the afternoon we would close so that we could go to church. Then we would wait anxiously for my dad to take us to the only local shop which would reopen after the church services and we would get fish fingers for tea.

The annual Wakes Weeks were another busy time in the salon. Virtually everywhere in Chorley would close down for two weeks. The mills, the factories and even most of the shops all closed down. We always had our newspapers delivered, but during these two weeks we had to walk across to nearby Mayfield Road and the paperboy would be there until he had sold out of his selection of morning and evening papers. Our comics were kept at Rigby's shop until normal service resumed. The town was dead during those two weeks.

On the Friday and the Saturday, I would stand on the front outside the shop and watch people pulling their suitcases down to the railway station or bus station as they headed off for the week to Blackpool, Great Yarmouth, Skegness or other seaside towns. Of course, they all had their hair done for going and would have had their appointments booked in with military precision, as anyone having a perm and a colour had to have them completed a week apart and then it would be a shampoo and set just before departure. Mainly, they went away for just one week and then a week of "days". The local coach companies would have a list a mile long of day trips and each day, people would go past dressed to the nines with their flasks and sandwiches, all set for the day out.

'Are you going away this year?' would be the burning question of the day.

'No, we're just having days,' would often be the reply.

Mum and Dad always kept the shop open the "first week", as it was known, and then for the "second week" and a few days after everyone had returned to work, we would go to Ireland to visit our relations, or "home", as Mum and Dad always called it. Elsie and Nora, two unmarried sisters who lived in Primrose Street just around the corner, would come to wave us off as we went for the ferry. They would be in tears as they would miss us so much. Ma Mullen would be out too and in later years, Mrs Canty, another of our pretend nanas, would be there. She was Irish, from County Sligo and had worked with my mum at Eaves Lane Hospital. She later moved into Primrose Street and would have a key in case there were any deliveries while we were away and to keep the plants watered. She was really good and would often clean the shop ready for my mum to reopen at the beginning of August. One year, we nearly didn't get away at all. Diane, who lived nearby, had forgotten that we were going away and just as we were about to lock the door to get into the car to go for the ferry, she arrived with a towel under her arm. Fortunately, my dad always allowed plenty of time for the journey, so my mum simply turned back and did Diane's shampoo and set. We just about made the boat in Liverpool for the overnight crossing to Dublin! It was considered good business practice to stagger our holidays, as no-one had any money when they came back, so we cashed in before they went and were ready for the trade when they were back on their financial feet.

Of course, Adrian and I would be at home for the school holidays and needed to be occupied. There was no daytime television or DVDs. I really don't know how I passed the time, but I would spend some time in the shop. Adrian would play with his toys and with his friends, and the time would just seem to go. In many ways, having Mum and Dad working at home kept us in order, although Adrian wasn't afraid to speak his mind sometimes, whereas I was much quieter. There was one occasion when my mum was glad that she knew exactly where he was when Audrey came rushing in one Friday night.

'I've just seen your Adrian in Primrose Street choking a cat!'

'I don't think so,' replied my mum, most perturbed that anyone could think he would do that.

In fact, he was in the sitting room watching *Thunderbirds*, having his customary sausage and beans for tea. There was a little boy with very blond hair just like Adrian who was often up to mischief.

But when Audrey was on the chair, Adrian got his own back. Looking up into her face as she was having her hair set, he blabbed, 'I don't know about having your hair done, missus, I think you could do with a shave.'

My mum was mortified, as Audrey had reached that age when some ladies acquire hair on their top lip and on their chin.

'What was that, love?' she was heard to say. Fortunately, she had removed her hearing aids so couldn't make out what he was saying, much to my mum's relief. Audrey went to Blackpool every year for the first week with her sister to the same boarding house and we always had a postcard within two days of her leaving, the postman bringing it long before she seemed to have had time to do anything other than say, 'weather great, food lovely.'

Even when we were away, my mum took her kit with her. My aunties in Ireland, my granny and numerous other people were always ready for a perm or even just a haircut. They weren't very well off, but then neither were we, but we still did it. They were good to us in return and we had many happy times, although we were often bribed with a visit to the toy shop before we set off into the Irish countryside to transform another relative. Then we would sit down to tea and homemade bread and jam, although Adrian always brought his own supply of sausage and beans.

Alice was always first to set off on holiday with her brother Wilf and his family. She had moved to Chorley from Wigan after the death of her husband and came every Saturday for years with her sister-in-law Mabel and her daughter Caroline. But one year she couldn't go away, as she was in Chorley Hospital having her gallstones removed. She brought them in a glass jar the following week to show everyone, but it was one holiday souvenir no-one wanted to see!

Two more Saturday regulars were Eva and Mary A, who lived next door to each other. They would go for "days" too. My dad called them Hinge and Brackett, as they came linking each other down Stratford Road, mainly because at the age of almost ninety, Mary was still tottering about in her high heels. She was always beautifully dressed, with coordinating earrings and flyaway glasses. She also had a glass eye. I only realised this when she dropped it one day in the shop as she was getting her purse out to pay. In all innocence, I bent down to pick it up and almost added it to my collection of marbles which were the current craze at primary school. I was very cautious after whenever a customer dropped something on the floor.

Although my mum had managed to have two babies and grow a new business, there was one hazard of hairdressing which nearly cost her livelihood. She had always had problems with her legs, and standing did not help. She developed ulcers on her legs, so bad that the doctor would visit on a regular basis. She promised him faithfully that she was resting daily for the three months prescribed. The truth of the matter was that once he had disappeared around the corner, she was back hairdressing. She was resting in a sort of a way; she took a stool in from the kitchen and rested the knee of her left leg on it while she moved it round the customer as she did their hair. This earned her the nickname "The Stork", after a margarine brand which was popular at the time. Despite being under the threat of having skin grafts and bed rest in hospital, by some miracle the ulcers healed in time and the stool was abandoned. It wasn't her last run in with leg ulcers and circulation problems, and it wasn't the last time that it almost cost her the job. Whenever I see trendy hairdressers resting on swivel stools while they cut someone's hair, I often wish such things had been around when my mum needed them most.

Chapter 8

The Seventies and Other Stories

The 1970s saw a number of changes. The shop grew from strength to strength, thanks to long hours and hard work, and we moved to a house rather than living over the shop. I started to help out on a regular basis, we started to expand into other retail areas and a lifelong affiliation to Blackburn Rovers began.

I was "minding the shop" one afternoon while my mum and dad went to an appointment. I was about fifteen at the time and I don't think it is the kind of thing that you would risk now. A man came into the shop and asked to speak to the owner.

'He's not here at the moment. Can I help?'

It turned out that he was from Blackburn Rovers Development Association and wanted to know if we would be interested in selling bingo tickets to raise money for Blackburn Rovers. My dad was a great football fan and, in his bus-driving days, had often taken fans to home matches to both Rovers and Preston North End. Fortunately, my dad came back and had a chat with him. He was a bit reluctant to commit.

'Come down to a reserve match for free and bring your little lad. You might find that you enjoy it and want to help.'

So that is what they did. Adrian quickly changed his Manchester United kit for the blue and white of Blackburn Rovers. Each Monday, they took a delivery of bingo tickets and they went like hot cakes. There were even a few winners, often small amounts, but it made their day. Sometimes they spent the money on another ticket in the hope that there would be a big win. This was long before the lottery and scratch cards were freely available, so it was a little treat along with their weekly hairdo. There was one major winner; Amy B won the vast sum of one hundred pounds, which was a lot of money at the time. So much so that both my dad and Amy had their photograph in the local paper and the Blackburn Rovers programme.

Soon my dad and Adrian were season ticket holders at Rovers. The only problem was that the shop was often open until after kick-off on a Saturday. A quick sandwich and a cup of tea was the order of the day, and I was often roped in to help with the last few customers as they dashed off to the match. Sometimes, my dad's mind was more focused on the possibility of a win than the customer.

'I didn't know you were having a change of hairstyle this week, Nora,' my mum commented one day.

'Neither did I,' she replied.

It seems my dad, in his haste to get away, had given Nora a fringe. Fortunately, she liked the new style and had it done like that every week.

The fundraising didn't stop at bingo tickets. My dad must have been one of the first recyclers known. At that time, old newspapers brought in much-needed cash. They were stored in the garage at the back of the shop and taken away in a large lorry every few weeks. A cheque would follow shortly for the Chorley Branch of the Blackburn Rovers Supporters Association, and eventually a presentation would be made to a Rovers player of the day at one of the fortnightly meetings which were held in the Townley Arms. Prior to the meeting, a number of the members would go out to the *Coronation Street*-style streets around the shop where people would leave out their newspapers for collection. Customers would also bring them when they had their hair done, and occasionally the shop door would open and a bag of papers would be deposited. It seems strange now at a time when millions are spent on just one footballer that at that time such paltry amounts were valued by the club and helped them in difficult financial times.

We moved from the shop in September 1971. We were growing up and I needed somewhere to do my homework and to study. But we seemed to spend as much time there sometimes as we did when we lived there. I was old enough to be left with Adrian, and on Saturdays and in the school holidays, we would get up at a reasonable hour and then go to the shop. I would help out and Adrian would play with his mates, as he still went to the same primary school and so would touch base in the living room, playing board games or going off for hours to play football. They would go home for lunch or I would take them to the chip shop and they would enjoy chip butties and carry on with their games.

In the meantime, it became my Saturday and holiday job to help out in the shop and brush up on my people skills. Many of my friends had jobs in cafes or hotels, but it seemed sensible that I should make an effort to learn the family trade, even though I was being encouraged to follow a more academic career. I transferred my skills from Glenis the doll and all her siblings to real customers. At first, I just took out rollers, swept up and answered the telephone. But I did graduate to perming some of the older clients, who either accepted that I would do it, including cutting, or my mum would let them have it at a cheaper rate. For this I was paid the grand total of fifty pence per week! That was my spending money, but I did manage to top it up with tips. These were especially welcome at Christmas, and as my mum and dad were finishing off on Christmas Eve, I would be off to Chorley market before it closed to spend my earnings on such delights as a red plastic handbag or a new quilted dressing gown. I remember buying a polo neck jumper with a belt for the huge sum of £1.50. Then we would be closed for a couple of days before the New Year rush began.

We also began to move into other retail areas. For some time, we had sold tights on a sale or return basis. A stand had been put in the shop and it was filled up on a regular basis and a small percentage from each pair sold was paid. Tights were really expensive when they were first developed and it took a while for ladies to change from stockings to tights. Later, we began to go to Manchester and buy our own tights, and I took charge of putting them on display and keeping them stocked up. But increased wages didn't come with increased responsibility. We also sold toys at Christmas and children's clothes. The shelf which had previously housed wigs was now a display area for radios and cassette recorders. We weren't very keen at getting up on cold winter Sunday mornings to go to the wholesalers, but there was always the coffee and toast to look forward to after we had stocked up. Maxi dresses were all the rage in the mid-1970s and we stocked those too. My mum and I found two lovely dresses to wear to the Blackburn Rovers dance, which was another fundraiser which was held once a year. I loved seeing all the new stock come in and the customers seemed to pick up all sorts of bargains for presents as well as rigging themselves out for a night at the club. We had some fantastic ladies' and children's clothes, and the extra money helped. When I went to college in 1974, I subsidised my grant by buying dolls and, using my skills at crochet, I used to dress them and sell them in the shop.

One of the biggest changes in the seventies was the change to decimal currency on February 15th 1971. There had been huge campaigns with posters and leaflets, and prices on the market and in the shops were often displayed in pounds, shillings and pence as well as the new currency. For the older customers, the change was not easy.

'I won't be bothering with that new money,' Ethel declared. 'I'll just pay the old way. After all, this new-fangled money will never take off until all us oldies die off.'

Somehow, my mum seemed to manage and still got paid each week. The mixture of old and new coins took some time to get used to and all the prices had to be converted. It took almost as long to take the cash as it did to get them on the chair sometimes.

There was also a big health campaign around that time which affected hairdressers. Headlice were prevalent and although my mum rarely saw it as a problem among her clients, if at all, she still agreed to take part. Some very colourful posters had been produced and these were distributed at regular intervals over a three-month period. These were duly placed in the window for all to see, with such eye-catching slogans as "Only twits put up with nits". My mum was staring out of the window on more than one occasion when she could see the response from passers-by. One old man, who didn't have a hair on his head, stopped, read the poster, scratched and moved on.

'I don't know why he's bothered,' my mum was heard to say to my dad. 'There's nowhere for them to nest on his head!'

Needless to say, both Adrian and I got the "just in case" treatment, as she always believed that prevention was better than cure. Despite living in a hairdressers and later teaching in primary schools, I have to say I have never had nits, so maybe there was method in her madness.

One of the most serious challenges of the early seventies was the three-day week. The crisis started in October 1973 when Arab states launched a surprise attack on Israel. The war in the Middle East quadrupled oil prices. Arab countries reduced supplies to the West. With the price of coal rising too and stocks dwindling, Britain's miners rejected a pay increase and voted to ballot for a national strike. On November 12th the miners and electricity workers began an overtime ban. Prime Minister Edward Heath declared that from January 1st 1974, there would be a three-day week for all industries and the use of electricity was to be cut to an absolute minimum in the home.

Of course, it affected the shop in that Mum and Dad had to rearrange all their clients, as electricity was only available during certain hours. It required some clever thinking. It was mainly sets, so they knew when they could use the power. So, ladies would arrive and have their hair washed and set and be lined up ready to go under the five dryers as soon as they were allowed. Then, the next five would be ready to go under. But with limited times when they could work, it was bound to have an effect on profits.

My mum seemed to be constantly troubled with varicose veins and leg ulcers. All that standing did little to help her circulation and it was during the late sixties and early seventies that she tried a new treatment. This involved having the veins injected, her legs heavily bandaged and a walk of three miles a day before she started work, rain, hail or shine otherwise the treatment would not work. It was a huge undertaking, but the alternative was surgery, which would have meant that she had to take time off work. Apart from this and the odd heavy cold or bout of flu, neither my mum nor my dad took time off work. They simply could not afford to, as they only made money in return for the service provided, and although the customers have been incredibly loyal over the years, it was a risk they could not take.

The trouble was that both legs needed treatment, so she went through it twice. How she managed to look after us, work long hours, walk three miles per day and carry on hairdressing is remarkable to say the least. But still hairdressing came first and she didn't miss a minute. At the start of the millennium, she was plagued again with leg ulcers. This time it did require hospital treatment, and in 2000 and 2001 she had bypasses in both legs in Bolton Hospital, which thankfully are still working today, helping her circulation. The vascular surgeon, Mr Ferguson, had her weighed up. Early one morning he came into the ward to see her, but she was in the bathroom.

'I suppose she's off doing someone's hair. I hear she styles half of Chorley,' he commented to Jackie, one of the vascular nurses who had been instrumental in persuading my mum that she really did need an operation and had visited her at home in every effort to get her ulcers to heal.

This time she had to stay off work. She was walking on a frame in the hospital after the first operation and I really didn't think she would be able to carry on working, but she gradually regained her strength and was off to the shop again – and her clients remained loyal, thank goodness.

In the 1970s, cut-and-blow-dry hairstyling was emerging. There were still many of the customers who wanted their traditional shampoo and set, but sleek, smoother styles were becoming more popular. My dad was the first to go off to Peter Collinge in Liverpool with a fellow Irishman, Sean, who was also a hairdresser in Chorley. They learnt all the latest techniques and my dad became the blow-dry expert in the salon, although he did practise on me and my mum before passing on the skills to his wife. Bobs were popular and the weekly magazine, *Hairdresser's Journal*, provided inspiration. Step-by-step guides to the latest styles appeared and helped to add to the salon repertoire.

One of the most popular styles around the mid-seventies was the Purdey cut. This was made popular by actress Joanna Lumley, who was the female star of *The New Avengers*. It was a brilliant style which was easy to keep, as long as you kept it trimmed and in shape. It was an updated version of the bob, and I plucked up courage to have mine done. It was the best style I ever had and was much admired. It was rather drastic, as I still had my hair quite long and it changed me overnight. It was around this time that I got my first teaching post in Chorley and I worked in the shop less and less but was always called upon to help out, even if I had just gone in to have my hair done. But there were children who knew who I was, as their mothers and grandmothers often came in to have their hair done. News soon went around that the new teacher was Margaret the hairdresser's daughter, and one of my first pupils was Sharon, Cath Murphy's daughter – the same Cath who had bought me baby dresses all those years ago!

Teaching was a very different profession in 1977 to what it is now. It was still demanding and there was lots of marking, but somehow the preparation was less vigorous and more generalised. It was a time when if you saw them making a Christmas decoration on *Blue Peter*, you could make it with your class the next day without having to consider if it was part of the curriculum, fitted in with your current theme or evaluate the children's performance beyond whether they had completed the task. Although you occasionally saw an inspector, the process was nothing like the vigorous Ofsted inspections which I experienced in later years and your most critical audience were the parents. Even the children were less vociferous! We had an hour and a half at lunchtime, and it was usual for most of the teachers, except for the head and the deputy head, to catch up on their marking, go shopping or even go home for a while, as most of them lived locally. I used to take my marking round to the shop and get on with it in front of the fire. Sometimes there would be some lunch prepared, but more often than not, I would have to make it for my mum and dad, as there was no such thing as a lunch hour for Margaret and Frank! Sometimes, I would be lucky enough to get my hair done, as it saved me going back after school, but it was always a quick do. I once joked that once I got in the door it was "eyeball to plughole", as Mum was busy and I only had so much time before I went back to school. The children often commented on my hair when I went back. I remember on one occasion I was fed up with my Farah Fawcett flicked-out style, so one Sunday we went up to the shop and she cut it all off and gave me a Judi Dench-type pixie cut. Some of the children hardly recognised me on Monday morning. It saved me having to sleep in those foam rollers which were popular at the time or put in heated rollers each morning. I don't know how I found the time, as in my later years of teaching, there was no time for that each morning.

Sometimes, the two worlds would collide. When my mum started doing ear piercing, I was her first victim. I had always wanted them doing but couldn't pluck up the courage. When they started to produce a gun, which put the gold studs straight in the earlobe, it became a popular service offered by hairdressers. Previously, you had to visit the jeweller, who would make the little holes with a needle. Girls in particular would pester their parents to have their ears pierced, but they took six weeks to heal up and the studs had to remain in place the whole time. Unfortunately, children weren't allowed to wear them for PE or when they went swimming. Schools eventually made the rule that they had to be done at the beginning of the summer holidays. However, some children decided otherwise. So, I would get a letter at school:

Dear Miss Sherlock,

Please excuse Tracy from PE and swimming for the next six

weeks as she can't take out her earrings.
Yours,
Tracy's mum

When I would question Tracy or whoever, the reply would nearly always be the same. 'It was your mum what did 'em, Miss!'

I would just have to hope that the head didn't find out.

On another occasion, I had my hair restyled into a bob which had a bit of lift in the back. I felt it took years off me, but one pupil soon put me right. 'I like your hair, Miss,' commented Amy, as she peered over my desk. 'My nan has her hair just like that but without as much "oomph" at the back.'

Working in local schools, everyone knew who I was, so when I moved three miles away, I thought I could be anonymous. However, on my first day as deputy headteacher, I was approached by Mrs Hicks, one of the lunchtime supervision staff.

'Now, Miss Sherlock, tell me. Am I right in thinking that you are Margaret the hairdresser's daughter?'

It seems that my mum had worked with her sister at Eaves Lane Hospital. Mary Hicks came right up to her ninetieth birthday and we would talk about people we knew and old times.

When we were doing a story about hairdressing, a small group of pupils, along with myself and Janet, the teaching assistant, turned up one morning at the salon and they tried out the dryers, gave change and watched as I had my hair washed and blow-dried. Of course, the rest of the staff thought it was just an excuse for me to get my hair done in school time, but we took lots of photographs to prove otherwise. We had a very enjoyable morning and turned it into a book. We even had a role-play area which I managed to set up with the help of my mum. It was lovely to watch the children take on the various roles and hear them ask the standard questions you expect, such

Margaret as a 15 year old apprentice in Aughnacloy County Tyrone

Frank and Margaret at their wedding on February 13th 1954

Linda aged four with her doll outside the shop.
Rocket Perms are on display in the window

Margaret and Adrian aged nine months outside the shop.
Notice the carefully styled curl!

The wedding of Derek and Barbara Latus at St George's Church Chorley on October 26th 1963. Linda is the little bridesmaid on the right

Walking day at Sacred Heart Church in 1966

Margaret, a reluctant Adrian, Linda and Frank outside St Joseph's
Church Chorley at the wedding of Cath and Pat Murphy Easter 1967

Margaret at work in the 1970s

Elsie Whittle, Vera Moss and Annie Downs walking with St Peter's Church Chorley in the late 1970s. They had all had their hair styled that morning by Margaret.

A rare photograph of Frank styling Margaret's hair on holiday in Ireland

Styling Sean McGonnell's hair in
Scotstown County Monaghan

Frank celebrating his 70th birthday,
always the Rovers fan!

The role play area at Anderton St Joseph's Primary school following the visit to Margaret's salon

*Frank and Margaret celebrating their Golden
Wedding on February 13th 2004*

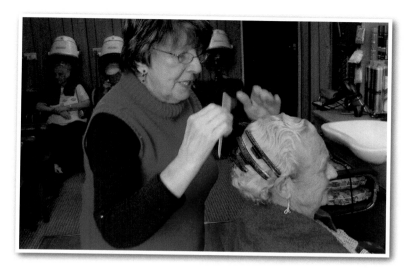

Elsie with her waves

BBC Radio Lancashire and North West Tonight presenter
Graham Liver receives the Margaret treatment

Eileen Walmsley, Graham Liver, Cath Murphy and
Margaret Cornwell celebrate 60 years in business in June 2016

Sheila with one of Graham Liver's much wanted shopping bags which he brought for everyone when he came to film for the Community Hero Awards ceremony

Cath Murphy, Adrian, Margaret and Linda at the BBC Radio Lancashire Community Hero Awards at Preston Guild Hall in September 2018 before she knew that she was the Overall Winner! (Photo courtesy of BBC Radio Lancashire)

Margaret with three members of International Singing Group
and 2014 Britain's Got Talent Winners Collabro who
presented her with her award
(Photo courtesy of BBC Radio Lancashire)

Rebecca Hall from Rosemere Cancer Foundation, Linda,
Margaret and Denis Ashcroft and some of the Thursday
supporters of the Back in Time in Music events

Ninetieth birthday celebrations May 2020

Ready for Action July 4th 2020

as enquiring about your holiday plans or asking you if you had any plans for a night out. At that time, we had to take lots of photographs for evidence of good and creative practice, and one of the dads commented to his wife one parents' evening, 'That Miss Sherlock is always changing her hairstyle.'

'That's because her mum is a hairdresser.'

As the pressures of my job took over, I suppose I spent less time at the shop than in previous years, but business went on as usual. Every night I would speak to my mum about her day and ask about the customers, and she would fill me in with the latest news and how everyone was doing. But there was one Tuesday morning when I was glad that I wasn't in the shop but wished that she had sent for me after the event.

It was just a normal day and the first customer was under the dryer and another was in the chair having a perm. Suddenly the door opened and two masked men came in and demanded that my mum open the till. To show that they meant business, one put a knife under Joan's throat and the other placed a knife under my mum's throat and demanded that she walk over to the till and open it. As it was the beginning of the day, she showed him that there was very little in the till. Joan pointed out that they were wasting their time. Fortunately, she worked in a betting shop so kept calm. With that, they realised that they were wasting their time and left. My mum immediately dialled 999 and within minutes, Stratford Road was like a scene from a television police drama. As they left, they were spotted making their getaway and another customer on her way to have her hair done saw what happened and pursued them on her scooter! Unfortunately, she lost them, but she was later able to describe them to the police. On the way home from my INSET day I noticed the headlines outside some of the newsagents: "Chorley Hairdresser Held Up at Knifepoint".

'How awful,' I thought as I drove past, but it was only when

I got home that I realised that it was my mum. She was on the telephone to Adrian, who by then was a solicitor in Blackpool. He was advising her that it was one thing to lie about her age to the press, but when being interviewed by the police it was a different story. She was all of sixty-four at the time, but she has always looked years younger than her actual age.

They were caught and my mum was front-page news when the *Chorley Guardian* came out the next day. When I went into school, the staff knew all about it. A huge arrangement of flowers arrived, as my Aunty Betty had picked up a copy of the *Lancashire Evening Post* from behind her door and had been shocked to read all about her hairdresser sister in Chorley. We had forgotten to ring up and tell her with everything which had happened. Radio Lancashire also turned up to record a piece for their morning programme.

'How did you feel when it was all happening?' she was asked live on air.

'Well, I was just worried that I wouldn't be able to go and see Daniel O'Donnell on Saturday. I have been looking forward to it!'

One of her customers wrote and told Daniel. There were gasps from the audience when he began to relate the story, but the theatre filled with laughter when she told them what she had said in the interview. He sang one of her favourite songs for her, so it turned into a night to remember.

Sometime later, I asked her what she did when she was waiting for the police to arrive.

'Well, I just carried on perming because I didn't want one side to be curlier than the other!'

It was a very frightening experience and one which none of us will ever forget.

Chapter 9

Dad

My dad, Frank, was an integral part of the business. He gave up his job at Hills' Bakery in the 1960s in order to help my mum. When the house next door came up for sale in 1963, Mum and Dad had the idea that they would buy it and convert it into two flats so at least they would have the rent. Dad was handy and could carry out most renovations and decorate, so it was his side-line. They later went on to buy other properties which he renovated and managed, so in effect he had two jobs! Mum taught him all she knew about hairdressing and he attended courses in Manchester and Liverpool. It was quite a novelty to have your hair styled by a man in Chorley in the 1960s and 1970s, but he soon settled in. It was handy to have him around to take myself and later Adrian to the local primary school. He enjoyed the banter and of course Blackburn Rovers was his favourite topic of conversation. I remember the big freeze of 1963 when he had to defrost the pipes using a blowtorch. Often, he would carry out renovation work at the shop working late into the night so that we didn't have to close.

Saturdays could be problematic, as he wanted to get away on time to the Rovers home games and even sometimes important away matches. I used to come in and help my mum as we stayed open to mid-afternoon, having started at the unearthly hour of seven in the morning come rain or shine.

It was in the mid-1990s when we began to notice that he was becoming less like his usual self. Dementia and Alzheimer's was not discussed as openly as it is nowadays and certainly everyone was less well informed. Like many people who have had parents who have suffered similarly, it was some time before we fully realised what the problem was and before we had a diagnosis. He had fallen from the roof of the car port where he kept his beloved motorhome and banged his head but failed to tell us until quite some time after the event. His doctor at the time asked if he had been in a car accident when they looked at the scans and we think this may have caused the dementia. In more recent times, it has come to light that professional footballers have gone on to develop memory loss as a result of heading the ball. But he lived another ten years after we were told, and he enjoyed "going to work" every day. Gradually he did less and less, but he enjoyed the company, and everyone was so kind and treated him so well. Quite how my mum managed, I will never know, especially in later years. He would potter in and out of the shop, and he enjoyed watching television and listening to the radio in the sitting room at the back. He even had a chair almost identical to the one at home, so to him he was at home. Sometimes he would fall asleep, but then someone would want to go to the toilet, which would wake him, and he would wonder where he was or what was happening. But soon he would be chatting away. Also, he quite liked the idea that my mum was making money!

In spring 2008, he developed a chest infection, but until a week before he passed away, he was at the shop. I remember the last morning I saw him setting off for "work". I was on my way to Sheffield, where I was working as an adviser three days each week, and I went around to see him before I set off. He was dressed as smartly as ever, thanks to my mum, in his shirt and tie, and apart from a slight cough, he seemed fine. When I came back on Thursday, it was clear that he had taken a turn for the worse and a week later he passed away in the early hours of May 2nd. We had closed the shop and we had all been with him all week at home. He had pneumonia and was eighty years old. We were inundated with cards and telephone calls. Gladys was one of the first to ring and Sylvia (the Toffee Lady), along with her husband Frank, came to visit us. The church was filled at his funeral, but for my mum and me it was business as usual the next day, even though we were both exhausted, but it is thanks to all of those people that we were able to carry on. We were also very thankful that for my mum's sake she had kept the business going through those challenging years, as she now had company and a purpose. I helped her for the first week and then it was back to the world of education.

Chapter 10

The Next Stage

After I went back to work, Mum carried on in the shop as before. She could drive and had taken charge of getting to and from the shop in the years when my dad had Alzheimer's, but she missed him greatly. Although she could now concentrate on the job in hand, it was the first time in over fifty years that she had been there on her own. Everyone kept her going and gradually she picked up the pieces of her life. The clients became more important to her than ever and many of them were widows too. She would urge anyone who was alone after the death of their husband or partner to think of all the others who were in the same position. It was fortunate that she had been able to keep the business going while looking after my dad, as she now had something to fill her time. I began to help more and more as I spent less time in the world of education and entered the world of hairdressing. Two years later, when Adrian was diagnosed with cancer and had to undergo extensive radiotherapy and chemotherapy, it was all our friends at the shop who kept both of us going.

Often, I would be drafted in when things became a bit hectic, as at first, she was reluctant to have anyone working with her, including me! I began to realise that often she wasn't getting a break for a cup of tea or a snatched lunch, even though she has never had a lunch hour in her life. Gradually, I began to appear more and more, mainly at the end of the week. Mum would go before eight o'clock for the first customers and I would appear later. Then I would leave her to finish off and she would close up at the end of the day. I really began to enjoy getting to know all her clients. Some I had known since I was a baby, but there were newer ones whom I hadn't met. I would answer the telephone and make tea and biscuits, which they hadn't had before as Mum just hadn't time except on the odd occasion. I would ring for taxis and make sure they got in the right one if two arrived at once. I experienced the friendly, community atmosphere of the shop and shared the ups and downs of the clients' lives.

My main bone of contention was that if my mum was ever under the weather, she would refuse to stay off as she couldn't let people down. On a couple of occasions, she had whatever virus was going around, but she would battle on or just have a couple of days off. Whenever I had to ring everyone, they were very understanding. On one occasion she had what I described as "a funny turn" and I really thought it was serious as she passed out. I rang the emergency services, fearing the worst. By the time they arrived she was back doing someone's hair! The paramedic checked her over and advised her to see her own doctor that afternoon, which I arranged. On each occasion, I would breathe a sigh of relief when she recovered and it was business as usual.

Bad weather was also a major headache. Christmas 2009 saw extremely heavy snow which froze. It was impossible to get my car out of the garage and the snow was so deep along the footpath at the shop that it was difficult to park, so we had to rely on taxis to take us to and from the shop. I was amazed at the lengths that people would go to in order to have their hair done. We had to pick our steps to get into the shop that year and in subsequent years, but the icy conditions seemed to hold no fear for many of the ladies. In fact, we had hardly any cancellations whenever it snowed. Before I started helping full time, I used to drop my mum off at the shop on icy mornings to save her having to drive. In the pitch-black darkness one Saturday morning shortly after seven, Jean Mather was stepping confidently towards the salon, having walked over a mile to get there at a time when she was in her early seventies. Mrs Fras from Whittle always came on alternate Tuesdays, usually on the bus, and as she lived out in the country, Mum would often try to dissuade her from coming out, as Tuesday was often a quiet day and it didn't seem worthwhile battling through the snow for one customer. Not only that, often the buses couldn't get through. However, if my mum dared to ring her the night before and suggest that the forecast wasn't good and offer to fit her in later in the week, it was met with disgust! Perhaps those who live in the country are hardier than most. Many a snowy Tuesday Mrs Fras waited for the bus and it didn't turn up, but someone would stop and offer her a lift and drop her in town. How she managed to walk the rest of the way without falling was a miracle. Gladys came one icy morning and had to be nearly carried in and out by the taxi driver. It seemed nothing would stop them.

Of course, waiting for a taxi to take us to work simply put my mum's blood pressure through the roof as she was so used to being independent. When one failed to turn up one morning, she gave them an earful on the telephone. That was one taxi firm I didn't dare ring again! When we arrived at the shop, the first customers were seeking shelter in each other's cars in order to keep warm and we had a backlog all morning. But I had to hand it to Maureen from Brown Street who, shortly after breaking her hip, was making her way on her frame down the middle of

Stratford Road one frosty Saturday morning just as daylight was dawning. At least we have a loyal clientele who never let us down.

Soon they all accepted that I was part of the scene and stopped asking for Margaret every time I answered the telephone. I took out rollers, sorted the towels and generally took care of the business side of things with help from my mum. Running a small business is more complex than most people realise. With ever increasing overheads, it became important to look around for the best deals in gas and electricity and telephone services. Of course, I wasn't on the payroll, but I was quite happy with my new voluntary role in exchange for a free hairdo once a week. The only trouble is that "Mummy's ladies", as I called them when I was little, take priority over me, and no matter how many times I put my name on the book, it invariably gets crossed off.

We also began to undertake some charity fundraising. When they had been open for twenty-five years, Mum and Dad raised some money for Eaves Lane Hospital, where she had once worked, in order to mark the occasion. Our neighbour, Denis, manages a singer from Lancaster called Sean Leonard. They travel all over the country performing, mainly sixties and seventies music with some country and Irish thrown in. So started the Back in Time in Music Nights at St Mary's Parish Centre. We sell tickets and those who can't attend like to buy raffle tickets. Margaret brought a large jar of copper which she had been collecting and asked if we would like it for our Rosemere Cancer Foundation Appeal. It all helps to swell the coffers and now we have a jar which I empty frequently. She also gave us some gold rings which we had auctioned, along with one from Eileen. Clients bring me prizes for the tombola which I run with Cath Murphy and by early 2019, with Denis at the helm, the grand total of almost twelve thousand pounds had been raised.

Sadly, as time goes on, there are the clients that you lose, not because they suddenly decide to go somewhere else to have their hair done but because they pass away. It is always very sad and in just a few months we lost Marjorie, Elsie (known as Wavy Elsie because of her finger waves) and Mrs Baxter, who wasn't able to come on a weekly basis due to mobility problems but supported Mum nonetheless. We were invited to all their funerals. We used to see Marjorie at mass at St Joseph's Chorley on Saturday nights and we would always admire her hair which had been styled that morning. Unfortunately, we couldn't go to Elsie's funeral, but Eileen did and brought us the order of service. Imagine our surprise when the photo on the front cover was one taken in the salon by me with my mum lurking in the background! We were always photographing Elsie, as she had such an unusual hairstyle as she liked her hair set in finger waves and she was always beautifully coordinated right up to her last visit three weeks before she passed away a few months before her ninety-seventh birthday. Although she had enjoyed good health well into her nineties, she had been unwell for some time, so we would make sure that she was warm and comfortable and even give her a hot water bottle in the wintertime.

'Stop fussing over me,' she would protest when I brought her tea and biscuits. She was often the last one on a Saturday and my mum would sit and chat to her while waiting for her daughter or granddaughter to collect her.

Ada Caddick came for as long as I could remember. She lived in Euxton and well into her eighties she thought nothing of walking the three miles to have her hair done on Saturdays, often coming via Morrisons where she did her shopping. In later years, her sons and her daughter, Susan, who was around my age and who I had known since I was a little girl, would bring her and come back for her. I went to her funeral and met with her family one last time. Eileen from Charnock Richard used to have her hair done every Saturday so that she could look her best for going dancing in Preston. She came right up until she had to move into a care home. Her partner, Bob, used to bring her in the final years and then he would go into Chorley to do his shopping while we took care of Eileen. He would come back and we would have a chat. Bob is always so cheerful. He was devoted to Eileen and visited her every day in the home even though it meant catching three buses.

So many lovely people have passed through the doors of the salon in my lifetime and really, they were our family and we still look on them as family and friends rather than clients.

Chapter 11

The Beginning of the End?

In the summer of 2015, the eerie silence of the darkened salon pierced my heart. I had just telephoned everyone to say that my mum was going to have to close for the foreseeable future. She had been fine until one Saturday morning when I got the fateful telephone call.

'Linda, I'm not going to be able to go to the shop today. I've got up ready to go and my arms are weak and I feel sick and shivery. I've tried to call Maureen, but she must have set off and you'll need to ring the others.'

Seeing that on the rare occasions she had been ill in the past I had spent hours negotiating with her to close even for a couple of days, I knew it was serious. She had been receiving treatment for an ulcer for some time and I had been warned that if she began to feel unwell like this to get her to the doctor straightaway so after some persuasion, we got her to the emergency doctor. He seemed baffled, muttered something about going into hospital which nearly gave both of us a heart attack, prescribed some antibiotics which made her worse and we set off for home. That night, I was convinced that she was going to die. I asked Adrian to stay over and I slept on the edge of the bed, fully dressed, thinking I would have to rush her off to hospital at any moment. She was burning up and twitching all night and the next day announced that she remembered nothing of it. If it was now, when we are all so much more aware of sepsis, I would have feared that was the problem. She seemed a little better and I took her to our own doctor on Monday. The general opinion was that it was some kind of virus and not linked to her ulcer. It didn't help that she was having a new bathroom that week and for the next four weeks! I moved in to stay with her. Two weeks later, she insisted that she returned, but she wasn't fit. She had no energy and then she did something to her back.

She battled on until one morning in October, when I realised that it was just madness. At quarter past six in the morning I was up and dolled up to the nines like I was appearing on breakfast TV and I went to get her ready. She could hardly put her foot to the floor as one ulcer had become five, she was very anaemic and had a bad back.

'I'll ring Gladys and the others for today and we will take it from there.'

It looked like the beginning of the end. I stood in the shop after making the final telephone call. Tears filled my eyes. Had I just closed the shop after all these years? The calls took ages and were harrowing. All her clients were upset and said such lovely things about her. Even they thought it was over. What followed was months of rehabilitation. Firstly, her back. Adrian and I escorted her into the waiting room of Fulwood Hall Hospital while she used a stick to help her balance. She paid to see a spinal consultant who ordered an MRI scan, but he painted a dismal picture. Later the same day, we returned to the same hospital and paid to see Mr Egun, a vascular surgeon. He took one look at her ulcers and looked horrified. He described one as "leg-threatening". He dressed them himself and she hobbled back to the car. Two days later, he arranged for his two vascular nurses to assess her legs and put them into compression bandages. We wheeled her back to the car and so began her rehabilitation.

It didn't help that she was having a new kitchen that week. All those years she was fit and well and we nagged her to have these things done, and we had chosen the worst possible time. The district nurses came every other day and then twice a week for the next fourteen weeks. The day after the bandages went on, she fainted. I thought she was dead and dialled 999. She was out for a few minutes but then insisted on telling me as she was lying on the floor that she was alright, but they still took her to be checked out. Her blood was so low that the doctor was concerned. We returned home and it was onwards and upwards from that day forward, albeit rather slowly. Some mornings she was shattered by the time she got downstairs and I encouraged her to have porridge for breakfast in the hope it would bring her back to full strength. She pestered the district nurses for a date when she could go back to her beloved shop.

'I bet you don't have many eighty-five-year-olds who ask you when they can go back to work!' I joked.

By Christmas she was able to go to church and by February, they were able to take off the bandages and her legs were healed. It was miraculous, as many people in their eighties who have ulcers never experience that moment. A week later, she returned to work. She went and had her hair done, applied her lipstick and got a new outfit. She went back looking like a million dollars and I had my first cold in ten years and looked like death warmed up. I did suggest that she phase herself back in, but of course that fell on deaf ears. Everybody wanted a perm. Some people had been to other hairdressers and declared that there was no-one like Margaret. Some had hung on until she got back, so it was a good job that she returned because we saw some desperate sights! Each day we filled the bin with hair. We took before-and-after pictures, and the transformations were phenomenal. Elsie cried as she was so happy to get her finger waves back as no-one else could do them. We heard tales of other hairdressers and were just glad that so many people had remained loyal. In her absence, some had visited, sent cards and gifts, but they were unanimous in welcoming Mum back.

Chapter 12

Celebrations

I had always been very secretive about my age. I knew there was one milestone birthday which was on the horizon and there would be no keeping this quiet, not if my plans to celebrate Mum's sixty years in business were to materialise. She was reluctant at first, as she had never been one to seek publicity; over the years, many people had said that to still be hairdressing in her eighties was a remarkable achievement and that we should contact the papers. I did write an article for a women's magazine about growing up in a hairdresser's salon in the 1960s, but that was about it. After her being so ill, I just felt that we had to do something to mark the occasion, so I set to work.

I wrote a piece for our local free paper, the *Chorley Citizen*, and within five minutes of pressing send, I had reporter Chris McGee on the telephone. It was a Friday afternoon and he commented that it was a lovely story and they would like to run it on Monday in their sister paper, the *Lancashire Telegraph*. He asked me to take some photos over the weekend to accompany the piece. Within minutes of arranging that and much to my relief, I had a call to say that a professional photographer could be at the shop within the hour if we could be there. As my mum tends to start early and finish early, we were in relaxation mode at that stage, so my mum, Adrian and myself had to rather hurriedly doll ourselves up and go to the photo session. Monday came and I knew it was in the paper by breakfast time when I got a call from a news agency in Leeds wanting the story to go national! The thought of that was rather scary, but after a family discussion, we decided to go ahead. Mum spoke to the reporter at length and I emailed him the piece I had written and the two combined soon hit the headlines… on the internet! Searching for a link to the local report to send to my cousin Dympna in Ireland, I was faced with the heading, "Is This Britain's Oldest Crimper?" My first thought was that she wouldn't like the reference to her age, but nonetheless it was very exciting.

Lots of people saw the write-up in the free paper and even in the national papers; the next stage was the radio. As avid listeners of BBC Radio Lancashire, I decided to contact breakfast show presenter Graham Liver to see if he would come to interview Mum and some of her long-established clients. He was doing a feature where he was looking for a new hobby called "Give it a try in July". I suggested that he should come and learn hairstyling from Britain's oldest crimper. Following some banter on air with his producer Leanne, she declared that it might be less of a hobby but more of a career change, but that he should visit "Hair by Margaret" anyway. The big event was set up for Thursday morning. Cupcakes were ordered, serviettes were bought, and my best tea set was packed up and the party was all set to go. Most of the Thursday regulars were long-standing clients, such as Jean Halton and her sister Jennifer, Cath Murphy, Margaret Cornwell and Eileen Walmsley. Gathered together in great anticipation, Graham duly knocked on the door and just went from person to person to get very natural interviews which went out the next morning. We were delighted when he joined us for refreshments.

'So which papers have been interested?' asked Graham. 'And what about the telly?'

Knowing that Graham was due to present our local news programme North West Tonight the following evening, I assured him that we wouldn't say no to the television cameras. But I was still quite surprised to receive a call on my mobile that evening from the BBC in Media City Salford. They were going to send their chief reporter, Dave Guest, to film the next day. I hadn't expected such a quick response, so we had to rearrange appointments so that we had at least an hour for the visit. The cups and saucers were quickly repacked straight from the dishwasher and we had to warn everyone and ask them if they would like to be on North West Tonight. Early the next morning, it was off to the cake shop again, only this time nothing had been ordered. Even the manageress in Greenhalgh's was bemused when I explained why I was there again and promised to tune in that night. Dave and his cameraman arrived on time, although I think he was expecting a town centre salon and not something tucked away in a quiet, residential corner of Chorley. But that is how businesses had been established in the past. When I was growing up, we had Billy Butcher's shop on the corner, two grocery shops, a hardware shop, a dress shop and a launderette nearby. I was amazed that we weren't thrown into rehearsals. Dave just asked me a few questions about why we were celebrating and I showed him the collection of photos which I had put together in a booklet to celebrate the sixty years in business. He simply snapped some of them using his phone while the cameraman set up.

He interviewed myself and Adrian, and I explained that I had been Mum's guinea pig over the years as she tried out every new style going, such as the Purdey cut and the Princess Diana while Adrian confessed to his Kevin Keegan-style curly perm. Various clients spoke on camera and were truly natural. Dave then proceeded to interview my mum and she waxed lyrical in her usual style for at least half an hour. I was beginning to think she could fill an entire programme and not just a five-minute slot. He picked up the story from when she was held up at knifepoint and everyone laughed when she explained that over twenty years earlier, she had simply carried on perming as she waited for the police to arrive.

We had a lovely little tea party yet again, and Dave and his cameraman joined us before rushing off to their next assignment. He commented how he loved doing these kinds of stories, as I know from watching the programme each evening that he has often had to cover the more tragic stories such as the Hillsborough inquiry, murder trials and tragic accidents, as he was the chief reporter on North West Tonight.

Of course, that night, we waited with bated breath, hoping that the report would go out. Unfortunately for us, Andy Murray had a major game of tennis which overran at Wimbledon so we clashed with *Coronation Street*, as the programme went out later than planned but we were delighted with the report which had been put together, including numerous photos with a particular focus on my various hairstyles. It was amazing how many people actually saw it that night and even now, people remember it. When we went to church on Saturday, one of the congregation nudged her husband and we heard her whisper, 'That's the hairdresser from the telly!' My friend Susan had also seen it and spoke to us at the back of the church. It was certainly our fifteen minutes of fame.

Around the same time, I received a call from the BBC in London from the radio producer of the evening programme which went out across the country. There had been a report that shampoos and sets were falling out of fashion. Now while my mum has a number of clients of all ages who have their hair blow-dried, she is one of the few hairdressers left who still styles hair in the traditional way. She went on live that night. Martin Logan, from the Sky programme *Out and About in Manchester*, contacted me, as he had seen my piece in one of the Irish papers. He came and filmed a longer piece and another great morning was enjoyed by all. This time, our relatives in Ireland were able to see the programme either on Sky or online, and as they repeated it several times at all hours of the night and day, many of them could see it. Graham Liver often rang my mum to discuss a variety of topics such as working beyond the usual retirement age and stress in the workplace. She has become quite a media queen!

Chapter 13

Clients and Friends

———————

There have been so many characters who have passed through the doorway at "Hair by Margaret", as it is now called, that it would be impossible to recall them all. But there are some that will remain in our memories for ever, especially the ones we got to know when I joined the business.

The Toffee Lady was always greeted with enthusiasm and brightened our Friday lunchtimes. Sylvia and Frank were devoted churchgoers. Sylvia is one of the kindest, most thoughtful people I have got to know when working in the shop. She always wrote the most beautiful, appreciative messages on our Christmas and Easter cards. She really enjoyed coming to have her hair done and she stayed a few hours, chatting to everyone and never complained if we kept her waiting. What is more, everyone got one of her famous toffees, usually chocolate caramels or, my favourites, dark chocolate mint creams. Every Maundy Thursday, she arrived with two Creme Eggs and on Christmas Eve, she went around with a box of Cadbury's Roses for everyone. Sylvia was the first to admit that she took a while to get going each morning and one day she shared with me her daily exercises which she carried out to get her going. When my dad passed away, Sylvia and Frank were among the first to call round to offer their condolences. In the wintertime, she always brought two sachets of soup to keep my mum and me going, and there have been a number of times when we have been glad of an instant warm-up. Each week, she somehow managed to acquire an extra copy of the *Citizen*, the free Chorley paper, which we passed on to someone who did not get one.

Even when she had a traumatic time, Sylvia approached it in her usual no-fuss fashion. Placing the newspaper, toffees and soup on the counter, she very quietly informed me that Frank was in the stroke ward. Sadly, he had taken ill the day before and was in hospital. But thanks to Sylvia's help, Frank was soon home and on the mend. Each week, we would ask about his progress and she would tell us how he was improving with the exercises which she had learnt from the physiotherapist and did them with him daily. At Christmas time, he helped her to make crackers for the Christmas Fair. One Friday, Sylvia told us that he had been told that he should give up driving. But everyone encouraged her to keep the car, as who knew what the future held. It was then that Julie announced that she too had endured a stroke ten years previously and none of us would ever have guessed. They both loved bird-watching, so one day, when he was on the mend, Sylvia suggested it was time to get back to normal.

'Get down that garden to your girls and get them fed!'

Little walks around the block led to longer trips to the local supermarket and soon the town was in reach. Sure enough, a few months later, Frank was back to driving around the town, although their annual trip to Weston-Super-Mare was off, only to be replaced by a coach trip to Llandudno. A couple of years later, Frank had to go into a home and Sylvia was lost without him, even though she received fantastic support from her son and her family and friends. We went to visit her at Christmas and brought her a Christmas plant and cards from the customers, and shortly afterwards, she was unwell and decided to join Frank in the home. Sadly, he has now passed away. The Toffee Lady is an inspiration to us all to share kindness and to remember those less fortunate than ourselves.

"Mummy's ladies" were numerous over the years, but one true lady was Lily Beesley. Except we never called her by her first name, as it would have seemed totally disrespectful. She lived around the corner from us and I can remember her from when I was a teenager, as my best friend's uncle lived next door. Lily and her husband, Jack, had Beesley's shoe shop in Chorley town centre with their son Michael. Lily's sister, Jennie, worked with her, but it was not really the kind of shop a teenager would visit, as they sold beautiful, high-class shoes, often with matching handbags. I remember going into the shop once with my mum and all the shoes were in boxes, neatly stacked. When you had described what you wanted or selected from the window or the display, Jennie or Lily would find them in your size and make sure that they were a perfect fit.

The two sisters were regular clients, early on a Saturday morning, having their hair done before going off to a day at the shop. When retirement came, the routine continued right up to the sad death of Jennie. Mrs Beesley became my mum's most senior client. Until shortly before her passing, she was very coy about her age but then admitted to the age of ninety-seven. If there was a recipe for living to a ripe old age, Mrs Beesley obviously had it, but I would put her longevity to three things: keeping slim, having a positive attitude and a family she adored. When I began to work in the shop, I got to know her better than I had over the years when I had bumped into her in town or when she was walking to collect her newspaper, as well as my fleeting visits to the salon when our paths might cross. Together with Jean and Marjorie, it had become the routine that once the three of them were under the dryer, I made the tea. This also meant my mum got a quick drink and her marmalade sandwich (quick to eat and digest) while I entertained them. Mrs Beesley never had a biscuit, although she did make an exception one day as her granddaughter was calling to take her into town on her way home. Her ninety-seventh birthday saw her granddaughter bringing the most exquisite, handmade cupcakes for the Saturday morning regulars. She was always telling us how lucky she was to have such a lovely, supportive family.

She had a wonderful turn of phrase and if anyone went to the toilet, she would always say, 'Are you off to water the flowers?'

When it came to paying, her favourite question was, 'Do you want a shilling?'

Whenever we would talk about anyone who had suffered a misfortune, she would sympathise with the words, 'It's a good job we don't know what's in front of us.'

So, it is easy to imagine how sad were all were just a couple of weeks later when she rang to say that she had fallen and banged her head and would need to cancel her appointment that week. We were even more upset when we heard that she had been taken to hospital a few days later and the prospects were not very positive.

'She'll rally round before long,' my mum, ever the optimist, assured everyone who asked about her, as she was known to many of the customers who came on other days of the week. We didn't even send a get-well card until we heard that she was on the mend, eating and chatting to her relatives. When things looked positive, I got a card and got lots of the customers to sign it. But the very day I took it round, a few hours later there was a knock at the door. It was her son Michael.

'I'm afraid it's not good news. Mum was going to be discharged today but in the early hours of this morning, they sent for us as she wasn't well at all.'

Disappointed that she might never read all the lovely messages which had been written for her, we expected the worst. Just a week later, I got a telephone call as I was getting ready to go to the shop.

'Linda, can you come up a bit earlier?' It was my mum. 'Eileen has come early and I've got Mrs Beesley here for a perm.'

I grabbed my keys and bag and set off, going over the words in my head as I drove. Did she really say Mrs Beesley? No. I must have got the wrong name.

'Look who I've got on the chair,' was the greeting as I opened the door. True to her word, there she was with half her hair in curlers. Marjorie and Jean were equally shocked when they arrived but nonetheless delighted to see her.

As she left with a headful of curls, she showed that she was well on her return to form when she said, 'I suppose you'll want a shilling.'

Mrs Beesley was back to her weekly visits for about three weeks after that and we noted how much stronger she was growing and we looked forward to resuming normal service.

But she fell again and this time, she moved into a nursing home not far from where she lived. Every week, customers would enquire about her and a quick telephone call to her son would give us the latest news. We really thought that it was the end of an era. Until one Saturday morning, the door flew open and I recognised Jackie, her daughter-in-law and in a wheelchair behind her was... Mrs Beesley!

'I thought I would give you a surprise. I need my hair done. They can do it in the home, but I said no. I want Margaret to do it.'

With the help of Jackie and to the delight of Marjorie and Jean, we were able to oblige, and the tea party was on once more with an extra cup for the helper.

'She was so excited about coming that she hasn't slept all night,' confided Jackie.

The visits continued until sadly Mrs Beesley was no longer on the chair on a Saturday morning and one snowy Wednesday morning, we attended her funeral at St Peter's Church, Chorley, which she had supported for a lifetime.

There must be something which makes some people feel that they get more than their shilling's worth when they come to Hair by Margaret.

The first time I met Connie, she told me off! I had only called into the shop to get my hair done and she was there for her usual Tuesday appointment. Connie was a dainty little lady who always looked immaculate. Living in a retirement bungalow yards from the shop, she often made her way there on her mobility scooter. She would be wearing an outfit rather than just clothes, complete with matching hat, gloves and bag. Sometimes she would arrive with her hair clipped 1940s-style or with her favourite Alice band, but she really preferred her hair to be permed and set, and she rarely missed her Tuesday treat. On this momentous first occasion, I picked up a towel which had spent all of about five seconds on a clean floor and put it on the back of the chair. We did not get off to a very good start as she felt it should be consigned to the wash bin.

All was well until about a year before her ninetieth birthday; she began to become less mobile and was prone to falling. She seemed to go from hospital to rehabilitation and she would insist on going back home again, which would last all of about a day before sadly she would fall again and the whole cycle would be repeated. We visited her regularly in Chorley Hospital and with her usually immaculate hair now at shoulder length, she convinced my mum that she could have her hair done on the ward! After checking with the nursing staff, we arrived one afternoon loaded up with everything to do a perm.

'But, Mum, she isn't well and I am not sure that she is fit to have a perm.' I panicked. 'I only agreed to come with you if you just did a quick wash and set.'

'Only if you want to have to go back next week and do it all again, only this time perm it because without a bit of curl her hair will be as straight as a die by tomorrow.'

So, we set ourselves up in the day room, where the light was good and there was plenty of room. We had just got going nicely when the door opened.

'Will you be much longer?' asked a very friendly nurse.

'Well, at least an hour and a half,' I informed her.

'I'm really sorry, but we are going to have to move you as we have a talk in this room for staff about end-of-life care.'

I really didn't fancy sitting in on that one, so we had to move to the bathroom. We managed to get Connie there and set up again. We had some very strange looks as we pushed her in a wheelchair and then I carried all the equipment. It wasn't the most pleasant of surroundings to do a mobile perm, but needs must; however, the whole process would have been much easier if we could have stayed put as promised. We managed to complete the task between us, with Mum doing the hard work and with me acting as the assistant. As time went on, it became apparent that Connie was now getting tired, despite the fact that she was determined that we carry on trying to make her look her best. At one stage, I got her a drink of water as we had to move her back to the day room, which was now vacant, as that was where we could plug in the hair dryer. Surprisingly, the perm turned out to be one of the best which she had ever had, but she was worn out.

'Is it frizzy?' she demanded when we had finished, in her usual blunt style.

We decided we had better get her back to bed, but there wasn't anyone to help us. Fortunately, we managed to flag down a passing physiotherapist who knew Connie and she very kindly got her into bed, as all she wanted to do was sleep!

We bid a hasty retreat back to the car.

'What will we do if we have finished her off and she dies tonight?' I panicked.

'Well, at least she'll go happy, as she has wanted her hair done for weeks,' replied my mum.

Fortunately, Connie lived to see more than another day and we even went back to hospital to help her to celebrate her ninetieth birthday, although she was now in a different ward, having been home and hospitalised a couple more times since her perm. In fact, she was now ready for another one! Eventually, she moved into a small and friendly home about half an hour away from Chorley. We would visit her on a Monday, but she really didn't like having her hair done by anyone other than my mum. So, she finally gave in and said again we would turn mobile hairdressers and go to do Connie a perm. This time it was so much easier, as we had worked out that we could complete it quite easily in her room without having to move her around.

'Don't do it too short, I don't want to look like Shirley Temple!'

So, my mum set to work and our second attempt at going mobile was much easier than the first. Connie looked lovely and we left her sitting up in her chair all smiles and we promised to visit soon again. In fact, we went on to visit her on numerous occasions in each of the seven homes which she then moved to, as she seemed to dislike them all. We always marked her birthday on April 1st and brought her something at Christmas. We had many a long chat, and one of the loveliest afternoons was at Christmas time when the children from the local nursery came to sing. It even brought a tear to my eye, and I had produced more Nativity plays, concerts and pantomimes than I care to remember! In between visits, she would write long letters on the lined notepaper which I bought her, as she didn't like the unlined fancy stuff. I always sent her a card if I went on holiday, as I used to think it would brighten her day, and I would find a card with a flower or a cute picture and write her a few lines in between visits. I always remember that we once brought her a present in a gift bag a few days before her birthday and she put it on display in her room, as she loved fancy things. Sometimes the carers would take her out shopping and she found beautiful clothes in Asda that I would never spot. In her last home, Connie made a friend and she seemed to settle down. On one of our visits, her last words to us were, 'I'm happy here.' I never thought I would hear Connie say that and sadly soon afterwards, my mum got a call to say that Connie had passed away. Ironically, shortly after there was a fashion feature on daytime TV saying that headbands had enjoyed a resurgence thanks to the Duchess of Cambridge. Connie would have been delighted to think that she was bang on trend.

Let us hope that she has found happiness in whatever home she is in now.

Sometimes you get a call out of the blue from someone who you think has forgotten that you are still in business. Such was the case with Mandy. Now I hadn't met Mandy, but I can remember my mum coming home one day and telling me she had to send a client home, even though she was booked in for a perm. Unfortunately, as it was an afternoon appointment, Mandy had called in at the pub for a few and rolled up drunk! When it was apparent that she was slurring her words, and could hardly stand up, my mum just had to get her out of the shop.

'I think you'd better go home and sober up,' was her advice.

'I think you're right, Margaret,' was the reply.

Mandy returned on several occasions after that and all was well, but it had been at least two years since we had seen her when she rang my mum at home one afternoon. I couldn't wait to meet her, and as she had been booked in for mid-morning, I was hoping that there wouldn't be a repeat of the previous incident. The door flew open and a shopping trolley came flying in, followed by Mandy in a long red coat with a black fur collar over a bright pink jumper, cut-off leggings and a pair of walking boots. Her hair was long and black and tied in a ponytail. After making herself at home, she duly informed us that she had called in at a hairdresser near to where she lived for a price for a perm. Having been told it would cost £60, she told them in no uncertain terms and a few choice words that she would not be availing of their services.

'I'm going to Margaret's, as she won't mess me about.'

Once we unravelled the ponytail, I was wishing my mum had quoted her slightly more than the standard £35, especially when I filled the bucket after three cutting sessions. Mandy kept us duly entertained throughout, as she occasionally burst into song interspersed with bursts of laughter. It transpired that Mandy was enrolled on a computer course at the local college and explained to us how to find information on the internet, alongside stories of her stints working in the kitchen of a care home and her charity shop work, all "placements", as Mandy preferred to call them.

Once she had her curlers in place, I disappeared off to make a cup of tea only to come back to find that she was about to light up her roll-your-own cigarette. As we no longer had customers who smoked, I had never before had to draw anyone's attention to the smoking ban in public buildings, but I had jumped the gun, as she was off to huddle outside for her smoke.

Mandy was a changed person, as she was highly delighted

with her Kevin Keegan-style perm, and she certainly looked younger and tidier. She was off to do her shopping, but not before she had given us a lesson in managing her finances.

'That's for't leccky and that's for me bus fare to college. Then there's me shopping on't market and Iceland.' She then waved another twenty-pound note and declared, 'And that's for me baccy.'

That was two weeks' worth of smokes. Rummaging in her bag, she then retrieved what looked like a watch box.

'And that's for vaping.'

Thinking that Mandy was attempting to give up the evil weed, I was about to praise her for her efforts when she announced, 'That's for when I can't be bothered rolling me own.'

Mandy bid us a cheery goodbye and went off into the winter sun to do her shopping. The two of us retreated to the back of the shop for a well-earned cup of tea.

In contrast, we have Eileen who comes every Thursday hail, rain or shine and always has a tale to tell. She may be in her eighties, but she has a fantastic memory for family dates and remembers the birthdays and anniversaries of those long gone. You can guarantee a lovely card from Eileen. She also has wonderful memories of working in the cotton mill and going dancing at the Tudor Dance Hall, where she met Eddie. She made a beautiful bride in 1960 and brought the photos to show us on one occasion. She is always very generous and she always has something for the tombola stall which I run with Cath Murphy at the Back in Time in Music nights which are organised by my neighbour Denis to raise funds for Rosemere Cancer Foundation. She very kindly gave us a gold ring which she had inherited and which we had valued and auctioned for the charity.

One day, she brought the most beautiful doll, carefully

wrapped up in an old shoe box. As usual, Eileen had a fascinating story to tell. When she was three years old, she contracted diphtheria and had to go in the local isolation hospital until she was well enough to return home. She took her favourite doll with her, but when she was leaving, the doll had to stay behind to prevent the spread of infection. In return, Eileen was given a pot baby doll, all dressed in peach, in the most beautifully handmade layette. Unfortunately, she was slightly damaged, so Denis and I set out to find someone who could restore her to her former glory. She had kindly donated her to us to auction for Rosemere, but I couldn't help but be touched by such a heart-warming story.

Perhaps the most unusual client we had was a Catholic nun! Sister Maria first came in the 1970s and, having been taught by nuns, I found it strange that she just walked in and hung up her wimple along with the other coats and hats. I am not even sure nuns were allowed to go to the hairdressers then, although I know times have changed more recently. She had her hair permed and set on a regular basis and even had it coloured. She was at teacher at St Catherine's Convent in Leyland, so she was delighted when I obtained my first teaching post in 1977. She was also from Ireland and when she retired and moved to Liverpool, we still kept in touch through letters and cards at Christmas and Easter. We were invited to her Jubilee mass and party when she returned to Leyland, and it was nice to see her, by which time I was considering retirement. Sadly, we later heard that she had passed away, but we will always remember her.

John is another exponent of the curly perm. He also performs at karaoke and has even been asked to sing in the clubs of various holiday resorts. He entertains us with songs and stories, and he looks years younger than his eighty years. It just goes to show that attitude plays such a large part in how people age. We do have those at the other end of the attitude spectrum. More recently, my mum was perming Lucy's hair.

'I'm eighty-five tomorrow, so my life is over!'

My mum and I looked at each other, and even though she has been coming for years, she obviously didn't realise how old my mum really was and despite being older, she was capable of perming her hair. It is quite sad when some clients talk about being glad that they haven't long to go as they see so many distressing changes in the world.

Chapter 14

A Night to Remember

I looked at my mobile as it rang out one night when we were watching TV round at my house. I decided to answer it, even though I didn't recognise the number.

'Is that Linda?'

I recognised the voice immediately. It was Graham Liver from BBC Radio Lancashire and North West Tonight. I thought he might want my mum to go on his breakfast programme the next morning, as since the sixtieth celebration we had been contacted on a couple of occasions if he was doing a feature about people working beyond retirement age or, on one occasion, to discuss why hairdressing was considered a less stressful profession than most. But he had a big secret.

I was aware of the first Community Hero Awards which Graham had been promoting on the programme. After a quick catchup, he told me that a team of judges had decided to give my mum the overall Community Hero Award for 2018. He invited us to a star-studded gala event at Preston Guild Hall on September 18th. He wanted to come and film my mum in the shop, but I couldn't tell her why he was back again. My mum happened to be at my house that evening and I had no idea how I was going to keep it from her. I went back into the sitting room to twenty questions.

'Who was that?'

I could hardly breathe, let alone speak, and I had to fight back the tears as I explained that we had been invited to the awards ceremony.

I was quite worried about how she would react on the night. It isn't easy to go up on a stage in front of five hundred people and I thought the shock might finish her off! We had great fun again when he came to film; the shop was filled, and they all spoke so naturally and so highly of my mum. He also interviewed myself and Adrian outside the shop. All we had to do was to keep mum until the big day. We were very excited on the evening and, accompanied by Cath Murphy and two other good friends, Denis and Sean, we set off. We had a lovely meal and we were delighted to be joined on our table by well-known presenter and talk show host Allan Beswick, who seemed to get on well with Adrian. There were nine awards on the night, all presented by various people, including the comedian Bobby Ball, one half of the famous Cannon and Ball comedy duo, and actor, comedian and radio presenter Ted Robbins. Ted has undertaken roles on numerous TV programmes such as *Coronation Street*, *Mount Pleasant* and *Benidorm*, among others. Top of the bill was the international singing group Collabro, who had won Britain's Got Talent in 2014. They are known for their faultless renditions of songs from the musicals. Graham had tipped me off that my mum's award would be straight after their performance, by which point she was all set for home, unaware of what was about to unfold. I cannot remember much about their performance as I was so nervous but they finished their set with "Somewhere" from *West Side Story*. My heart was beating fast as Graham announced that there was one more winner who was oblivious to the fact that they were about to be awarded. With that, the shop appeared on the big screen and according to Adrian, my mum's jaw dropped in disbelief. The next thing I heard was, 'And the winner of the Community Hero Award 2018 is Margaret Sherlock.'

The spotlight was on the three of us as we escorted my mum up onto the stage. It was only later that I realised that the whole audience of five hundred nominees, celebrities and guests were giving her a standing ovation, shouting and cheering. We let Mum take centre stage with Collabro, who gave her the award. She was interviewed by Graham and she performed like a star. I was amazed and I needn't have worried, as she took it all in her stride. Next, we were ushered off for photographs with Collabro and then someone asked us to wait at our table as Graham wanted to interview us for the breakfast show the next day. It had been a fantastic night, but there was more to come.

As we left the hall, Adrian went to bring the car round. Everyone was saying, 'Well done,' and, 'Congratulations.' A lovely lady approached us and asked my mum if she would like to have her photograph taken with her husband, who turned out to be Chorley MP Sir Lindsay Hoyle and now Speaker of the House of Commons. We had a chat with him and with Chorley Councillor, Alistair Bradley, and photos were taken. Sir Lindsay later wrote about my mum in his column in the *Chorley Guardian* and he called her "an inspiration". Once again, she had hit the headlines. We went home on a high and it will be a night we will always remember. Of course, we were then able to share the secret with everyone and explain why they had been filmed once again.

Chapter 15

And So It Goes On

When the Community Hero Awards for 2019 were announced, Mum was back on Radio Lancashire again. This time we had a visit from Phil Cunliffe, who was in Chorley encouraging people to nominate people worthy of an award. It brought back such lovely memories of a night to remember as she told Phil about how she had received a letter from Senator Robbie Gallagher from her hometown of Monaghan in Southern Ireland. I had written a piece for the local newspaper, the *Northern Standard*, and sent if off with a photo, as I felt it was the best way to share the good news with our many relatives and friends in the area. I keep in touch with some of them via email and WhatsApp, but there were many more that it was more difficult to reach.

In the year following the award, as well as our regulars, we had some new customers. In the very week that Connie, whom we had visited in numerous homes and had styled her hair in Chorley Hospital, sadly passed away, a new Connie came into our lives, having moved from West Bromwich to Chorley in order to live nearer to her daughter. Her son-in-law Pete had

seen a feature in *Local Life*, a monthly glossy magazine delivered
to homes in Chorley and decided that my mum would be the
perfect hairdresser for Connie. She is a lovely lady and arrives
every Friday morning. We have also got to know her family. A
couple of years earlier, Sheila had moved into the bungalows
near the shop and her grandson, Charlie, had spotted the shop
and suggested that it would be a good place for her to have her
hair done. She, too, is from Ireland, so we have a lot in common.
I often joke that when she walked in that day that she didn't
know what she was letting herself in for, as she has been on
television with us and featured in the video which they showed
at the Community Hero Awards. Sometimes, we may have
extra clients in when she arrives for her appointment, but she
just joins in with the chat and enjoys the company. New clients
soon become friends and realise that they have stumbled upon
a salon which is unique.

Some days you can set your watch by the regulars, like the
Thursday gang including Eileen, who is a relative newcomer
of fifteen years, yet now one of the family. Jennifer still has a
beautiful head of hair without a hair out of place, despite her
sister Jean's warnings of the perils of Belair lacquer, but she
still likes her hairspray. Only recently, I was telling Jean how
I remember her warning me when I was just seventeen. I had
bought a 1970s-style maxi dress to wear and I was catching the
bus to Preston one night to meet some of my friends for a meal.
She told me to be careful standing at bus stops. In my innocence,
I didn't really know why.

'But you do now!' She laughed as I recalled the event some
forty-seven years later.

Margaret, whose idea it was that we should collect loose
coins for the Rosemere Cancer Foundation, never misses an
appointment and I often remind her of her late mother who
worked on a pot stall on the Flat Iron market in Chorley. She

brought me a Beatles mug and a George Best mug in the 1960s. If only I had kept them instead of having my tea from them each morning before school. Margaret is a skilled gardener, unlike myself, but recently she brought me details of a garden design company who have now built a garden to be proud of at the side of my house. I joked that Margaret should come and cut the ribbon! Cath Murphy is now a grandma and we enjoy many a good night out. Denis, my neighbour and now family friend, always calls. He is there to give Eileen a lift into town after filling us in on the latest news and having a cup of tea. On a good day he even brings us all cake or chocolates! They are some of our most fervent supporters of the Charity nights which Denis organises twice a year in aid of Rosemere, where Adrian was treated successfully in 2010. Fridays we have Mr and Mrs Almond, fellow retired teachers, among other regulars.

Then we have the ones who come every few weeks, such as Derek and Steve the Blackburn Rovers fan, now retired, but he has been having his hair cut since he was a teenager and recently had his hair cut for his son's wedding. He was one of the gang who used to go out on a Monday night collecting newspapers for Blackburn Rovers. Bob used to live around the corner but always comes to have his hair cut. Carol has been coming since she was at school. Her mother, Phyllis, came every week and had her hair in a French roll for many years. When I was twenty-one, she gave me the equivalent of twenty-one shillings, one for every year of my life. I put it with some other money which I had been given and bought a bracelet which I still treasure. Only recently, Carol was laughing as she realised that my mum did her hair when she was at primary school and she is still using a comb which she bought from my mum when she was at secondary school. Mum has seen her get married, have children, become a widow and enjoy her grandchildren. Still she wouldn't have her hair done anywhere else. Marion comes every third Wednesday. Cath Murphy is just one who had a wash and set for her wedding and a cut and blow-dry for her golden wedding fifty years later. Kathleen had her hair done for her wedding in the 1960s and then my mum lost track of her until one day we bumped into her in Aldi. She now has a regular appointment. There is Ivy and Mrs Hull, who do their own hair in between salon visits.

Our most senior client, Elsie, sadly passed away quite recently. Sylvia, the Toffee Lady, nicknamed her "Wavy Elsie" because she liked her hair in *Downton Abbey*-style finger waves. She reckoned my mum was the only hairdresser left who can do them because she remembers learning how to do them first time around. We keep in touch with Elsie's family, as her daughter-in-law Ann is also a client. We were really upset when Michael Cheston passed away suddenly. It was like we had lost a member of our own family. He would bring his wife Barbara to have her hair done and he would have his cut too. He called in every Saturday morning on the way to the supermarket and he would bring magazines for the clients to read while they were having their hair done. He was such a kind person.

Then there's Jean, Jennifer's sister, who delights us with tales of times gone by and life in Chorley during the war years. She was one of my mum's first clients and has been to every hairdresser in Chorley and some beyond, but she always came back and filled my mum in with details as to how the others worked. Her brother Frank now walks down with her every Saturday morning on his way to see another sister and client, Eveleen. He was only six years old when Jean first started coming to have her hair done and he recently celebrated his seventieth birthday by bringing us some birthday cake after we had sent him a card. Everyone is always welcome, no matter when they ring for an appointment.

In my lifetime, hundreds of people have crossed the threshold. The salon started off as "Margaret's" and then became "Margaret and Frank". Now it is officially "Hair by Margaret", but everyone still refers to it as "Margaret's". People will often come in, and then when they tell friends where they go to have their hair done, they will say, 'Is she still there?'

When Judy came for the first time a few years ago, having moved back to the area, she commented that she used to know a Margaret years ago who did hair in the same salon.

'It's me,' my mum replied, much to Judy's amazement and amusement.

I often wonder how my mum has managed to sustain a business for sixty-four years. The only place she has ever advertised is in St Peter's Church Magazine, not because she needs to but in memory of Mrs Beesley, who first asked many years ago if she would support the fundraising. Her success has been due to word of mouth, good service, always putting others before herself and one hundred per cent enjoyment in her work. Even now, she is ready to go every morning and cannot wait to get there. I don't think many people can say that at the age of eighty-nine!

I suppose Connie, one of our new ladies, summed it up one day as she was leaving: 'I look forward to coming here. You always cheer me up.'

Another new friend is Dorothy, who told us one day how she was explaining to her husband that she had settled in with her new hairdresser as she gets her hair done, has a chat, gets a cup of tea with biscuits and the latest magazines. Gladys, one of Mum's first customers, moved away a few years ago to be nearer to her family. She often rings up for a chat and they like to keep in touch. Sometimes I look round at the shop and realise that it bears little resemblance to the glossy salons found throughout the country, but I think that is the appeal. If we had realised twenty years ago that Mum would still be there in 2020, we would have carried out renovations, but she was beyond retirement age even then!

At the end of the day, Margaret has the satisfaction of a job well done and the knowledge she has spread a little happiness along the way.

Chapter 16
And Then This Happened

That was where the story was supposed to end. Everything was going along well, with everyone coming for their regular weekly appointments and looking forward to the spring of 2020. The rain had been torrential most days and small notices were beginning to appear on shop windows and public buildings about a virus which was spreading in China and asking anyone with symptoms to stay away. But Thursday February 20th 2020 was about to mark the beginning of massive changes in our lives as a family and that of our clients.

As it was raining heavily and being in a hurry to get to the shop, Mum decided to come out of the back door and meet me at the car instead of waiting for me to lock up and take her heavy shopping bag. As I approached the door, I saw her slip and fall head over heels out of the back door. Rushing towards her in the pouring rain, already I could see a huge bump on her forehead. Her bag was lying in the yard – the *Chorley Guardian*, which many people enjoyed reading under the dryer, was reduced to pulp. A packet of biscuits and a box of tea were lying in a puddle, and for a moment I didn't know what to do for the best. I ran to the car for my mobile and rang Adrian, who was with us in a matter of minutes. In the meantime, the rain lashed down on both of us as I tried to establish if she had broken any bones. She kept squeezing her left hand and when Adrian arrived, we managed to help her into the house and convinced her that she needed to go to hospital. Her main concern was that her coat and shoes were wet, and she insisted on changing.

'It's not a fashion parade!' I heard Adrian say.

As he helped to get her ready, I rang the first two clients to say that we wouldn't be there for them that morning.

At Chorley Hospital she was seen quickly by the triage nurse and took her place in the waiting area with a number of other people who had also slipped on the way to work, given the atrocious weather conditions. Meanwhile, I rang the others to say that we were at the hospital. Eventually she saw a lovely consultant, who was amazed at her age and the fact that she was still working, which is not an unusual response from the medical profession. He assured her that, as she hadn't been knocked out that a scan wasn't necessary, but he sent her for an X-ray on her left wrist. All this happened very quickly and I cannot praise the staff enough for the attention she received that morning. On our return, the doctor informed us that she had broken her wrist but fortunately it wasn't a bad break and could be manipulated back into place without the need for anaesthetic. We looked at each other and I could read her mind.

She would have to close the salon.

She was put into plaster for six weeks and had a very tasteful and quite light red cast which matched most of her outfits. I moved in with her and Adrian came each day to help. As promised by the doctor, the next day she had a black eye which made her look as if she had encountered two-time heavyweight champion boxer Tyson Fury! Her leg ulcers showed signs of breaking out, which was a bigger worry than her broken wrist.

Thanks to vascular surgeon Mr Egun, whom we saw at Fulwood Hall Hospital, his fantastic vascular nurses at Royal Preston Hospital and the district nurses in Chorley, the ulcers healed quickly.

However, there was a bigger problem on the horizon which was to affect the whole world. Coronavirus, or Covid-19, was creeping into our lives. By March 23rd 2020 we were in lockdown. It took a while for my mum to realise that all hairdressers would be closed for the foreseeable future, along with other non-essential shops and businesses and we would all have to "Stay Home, Protect the NHS, Save Lives". Most of our clients had been waiting for us to reopen rather than going to another salon and we were very grateful for their loyalty. My mum had kept in touch by telephone and some had even been round with get-well cards and presents. It gave Mum a longer time to recover and she eventually had her plaster removed at the beginning of April. It was during lockdown that I began to realise that it can be an advantage to have a mum who is a hairdresser, as when even celebrities were bemoaning the fact that they couldn't get their hair done, Adrian and I had our own personal stylist, even if it was in the kitchen! Shortly before her ninetieth birthday on May 5th, the Prime Minister Boris Johnson announced that he hoped that hair salons could reopen on July 4th and so that date became firmly imprinted in her mind.

Her special birthday in lockdown was a lovely occasion, despite what was going on outside in the wider world. All along she had insisted that she wanted to ignore the occasion completely and I would have loved her to have been in the salon on the big day, but it wasn't to be. The day started with a telephone call from BBC Radio Lancashire's Graham Liver as he interviewed her live on air and recalled his past encounters with her. Later in the day, thanks to my friend Mary in Northern Ireland and her sister-in-law Karen, a personalised video message from international Irish singer Daniel O'Donnell arrived on my phone. That evening we had a special tea, but the spectacular cake which I had in mind couldn't be sourced, so a smaller version was enjoyed. Adrian suggested that we send a photo to the *Chorley Guardian*, along with a report, and Mum agreed. This was picked up by a news agency and once again, Mum's remarkable story was online. We also received a telephone call from the *Belfast Telegraph*. The next day Mary informed me that Mum was on the front page, along with Cath Murphy, and a more detailed feature inside with the story of how she had started out in Northern Ireland in 1945. She sent us pictures of the article, which I forwarded to my various friends and relatives, and my cousin Anna was able to get a copy while out shopping. Ivy rang to say that her sister in Lisburn had also spotted the article and rang to see if she knew the hairdresser in question! As she had been doing her hair more years than we all cared to remember, she was able to fill her in. Later Ken Murphy, who has always carried out jobs both at home and at the shop, had received a similar call from his brother in Northern Ireland. Later in the summer, Mum was also delighted to receive a telephone call from one of Mrs Nesbitt's sons, Christopher, who by sheer chance had bought the newspaper that day as somehow the photograph had caught his eye. He was amazed to read that this was one of his mother's apprentices from 1945. It really is a small world.

I did have my doubts as to whether we would be able to reopen in July if we got the go-ahead. After all, most people over seventy years old hadn't been out for weeks and some had been told to shield for twelve weeks. However, Mum was determined. Adrian felt it could be the making of her and by day four of her return, I could see that he was right. She just comes alive in the salon and at home she was just waiting to get back to all her clients. Having said that, I really do not know how she stood the pace, as I was worn out just keeping things ticking over. She was the one with the challenging job of getting everyone looking good again.

There were a lot of preparations before we could go back. Following guidance from the government and the National Hair and Beauty Federation, we set to getting the salon ready for reopening. The three of us cleaned from top to bottom. I had prepared notices which needed to be displayed and Adrian helped to measure out our two-metre distances, which involved removing some furniture from the salon. I also had to source disposable capes and aprons along with the visors which we were required to wear. Of course, we had to set up a sanitising station along with additional cleaning equipment, as everywhere had to be made safe between each client. We spent the best part of a day contacting clients, who were delighted to hear that we were reopening. In order to make it fair, we decided to open extra days and for longer hours and take people forward in turn from their usual days.

On Saturday July 4th 2020, we arrived with a mixture of nerves and excitement. Our first client was Jean Halton.

'What do you two look like?' she greeted us as we opened the door. 'You look like you've come from space!'

She was desperate for a perm and Cath Murphy looked different after her long-awaited colour cut and blow-dry. We had to allow longer for each appointment as some clients needed their hair cutting three times before Mum could get it back into shape. It became like Groundhog Day, as we turned up each day, worked longer hours and got used to our visors and new way of working in a hairdressing salon. By week two, our weekly clients were reporting back how delighted they were to get their hair done and how much it had brightened their lives. Many of them were still staying at home, as they were wary of going into shops, so we were delighted that they felt that they could rely on us to keep them safe and well groomed. Instead of dishing out tea and biscuits and the latest magazines, I had to concentrate my efforts on bleaching and disinfecting. The policy on mask-wearing changed three times in the first six weeks. Firstly, clients didn't need them, but we had to wear visors. Then they were advisable for clients before becoming mandatory. That was another task for us to monitor, although most people were very good at wearing and managing their face masks. Finally, at twenty-four hours' notice, I learnt that my mum and I had to wear medical-quality masks as well as visors!

After an initial few weeks, Mum managed to get everyone's hair in order and soon we were welcoming those who had been required to shield for longer. We were tired but experienced great job satisfaction. It is amazing what effect a haircut can have on people's lives and to see the smiles on their faces was worth all the effort. Many of them were worried about Covid-19.

'I wish it would go away.'

'I will be glad when it is over.'

'I don't know what we will do when Margaret retires.'

'It won't always be dark at seven!' was a more optimistic comment from eighty-nine-year-old Jean, who got the saying from her grandma.

Eileen was telling us one Thursday morning that the taxi driver, now in his forties, had his ears pierced by my mum when he was a teenager.

'Is Margaret still going?' he asked in amazement.

'Tell him next time that I'm not going anywhere.'

Although no-one knows what the future holds, my mum still has no intention of hanging up her scissors and retiring, even at ninety!

About the Author

Linda Sherlock made her first visit to the hairdressing salon at just ten days old. As a teenager, she worked in her mum and dad's salon as a trainee hairdresser on Saturdays and in the holidays for fifty pence a week plus tips. She pursued a career in education as a Deputy Headteacher, Acting Headteacher, Primary English Teacher Adviser and Teaching and Learning Consultant. Now her life has come full circle as she re-joined the business on a part-time basis in 2010 as Business Manager, helping her mum, Margaret, with everything but the hairstyling. Linda has contributed to a number of magazines and publications, including academic journals. Her monologue, *The Exile's Child*, was performed and recorded by the Green Curtain Theatre Company, London, in January 2019, and her writing has been featured by the BBC. Linda has a Masters degree in Educational Research and she is a member of Chorley and District Writers' Circle.